CAMPAIGN 296

MILVIAN BRIDGE AD 312

Constantine's battle for Empire and Faith

ROSS COWAN ILLUSTRATED BY SEÁN Ó'BRÓGÁIN
Series editor Marcus Cowper

First published in Great Britain in 2016 by Osprey Publishing,
PO Box 883, Oxford, OX1 9PL, UK
1385 Broadway, 5th Floor, New York, NY 10018, USA
E-mail: info@ospreypublishing.com

© 2016 Osprey Publishing Ltd
OSPREY PUBLISHING IS PART OF BLOOMSBURY PUBLISHING PLC

All rights reserved. Apart from any fair dealing for the purpose of private study, research, criticism or review, as permitted under the Copyright, Designs and Patents Act, 1988, no part of this publication may be reproduced, stored in a retrieval system, or transmitted in any form or by any means, electronic, electrical, chemical, mechanical, optical, photocopying, recording or otherwise, without the prior written permission of the copyright owner. Enquiries should be addressed to the Publishers.

A CIP catalogue record for this book is available from the British Library.

ISBN: 978 1 4728 1381 7
PDF e-book ISBN: 978 1 4728 1382 4
e-Pub ISBN: 978 1 4728 1383 1

Editorial by Ilios Publishing Ltd, Oxford, UK (www.iliospublishing.com)
Index by Sandra Shotter
Typeset in Myriad Pro and Sabon
Maps by Bounford.com
3D bird's-eye views by The Black Spot
Battlescene illustrations by
Originated by PDQ Media, Bungay, UK
Printed in China through Worldprint Ltd.

16 17 18 19 20   10 9 8 7 6 5 4 3 2 1

ACKNOWLEDGEMENTS

Thanks to all those who made photographic material available for reproduction. Special thanks to the Cowan family, Dr Duncan B. Campbell, Marcus Cowper, Dr Florian Himmler, Thomas McGrory, Seán O'Brógáin, Steven D. P. Richardson, and to novelist Ian Ross for enlightening discussions about Constantine's army and campaigns.

ARTIST'S NOTE

Readers may care to note that the original paintings from which the color plates in this book were prepared are available for private sale. The Publishers retain all reproduction copyright whatsoever. All enquiries should be addressed to:

seanobrogain@yahoo.ie

The Publishers regret that they can enter into no correspondence upon this matter.

THE WOODLAND TRUST

Osprey Publishing are supporting the Woodland Trust, the UK's leading woodland conservation charity, by funding the dedication of trees.

CONTENTS

ORIGINS OF THE CAMPAIGN 5
The imperial college . Augustus and *Princeps* . Italy invaded . Alexander and Licinius . Maximian's treachery and Constantine's vision . The death of Galerius

CHRONOLOGY 16

OPPOSING FORCES 17
Constantine's army . Maxentius' army . Tactical organization

OPPOSING COMMANDERS AND PLANS 32
Constantine . Maxentius

THE CAMPAIGN 34
Segusio to Augusta Taurinorum . Brixia and Verona . The advance on Rome

THE BATTLE 44
Primary sources . Tor di Quinto and the archaeology of the Milvian Bridge region . The battle of the Milvian Bridge: a tentative reconstruction . Rout

AFTERMATH 86
Praetorians and Horse Guards . Constantine enters Rome

THE BATTLEFIELD TODAY 90

BIBLIOGRAPHY 92

ABBREVIATIONS 93

INDEX 95

The Roman Empire in AD 312

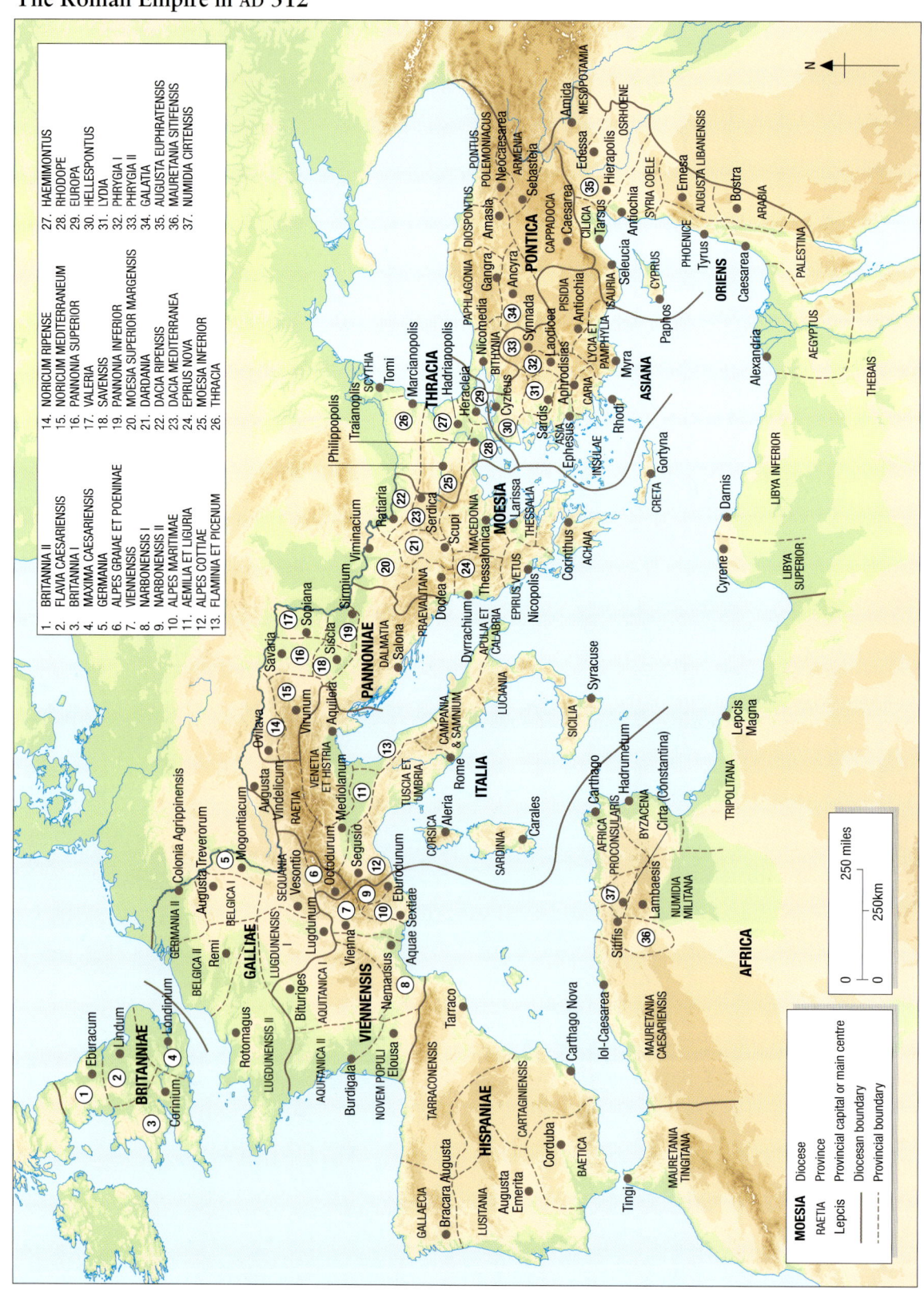

ORIGINS OF THE CAMPAIGN

Sources: *Pan. Lat.* 10(2), 11(3), 8(5), 9(4), 7(6), 6(7), 5(8), 12(9), 4(10); Lact. *DMP* 7–43; Euseb. *HE* 8.16–17, *VC* 1.18–32; Zos. 2.7–14; Aur. Vict. 39–40; *Epit.* 39–41; *Origo* 1.1–4.13; Eutrop. 9.19–10.5; *Chr. Min.* I 148.

THE IMPERIAL COLLEGE

On 20 November AD 303, Diocletian celebrated his *vicennalia*, the start of his 20th year of rule, in Rome. At his side was Maximian, loyal comrade and fellow-emperor. Despite his title of Augustus (senior emperor), Maximian was very much the junior in their imperial partnership. Also in the imperial retinue was the tribune Constantine. He was the ambitious son of Constantius, the Caesar (junior emperor) Diocletian had appointed in AD 293 as Maximian's nominal subordinate and heir in the western half of the Empire. In that year, Constantine had been sent to Diocletian's court at Nicomedia (Izmit) and for the next ten years served at the right hand of Diocletian, or his Caesar, Galerius. As the eldest son of a Caesar, Constantine was evidently being groomed to enter the imperial college.

Diocletian and Galerius, Maximian and Constantius, the original Tetrarchs. The *concordia* of Diocletian's imperial college did not survive his abdication in AD 305. (A. Haye)

It was fitting that the man who had brought the Roman Empire out of the great crisis of the 3rd century AD, stabilized its frontiers and reminded Germans, Sarmatians and Persians of the might of Rome, celebrated the start of his 20th year of rule in the City of the Caesars. However, Diocletian did not like Rome or its rowdy populace and soon withdrew for Ravenna, where he assumed the consulship of AD 304. He then travelled east towards Nicomedia but was struck down by a debilitating illness. He recovered but could no longer face the burden of rule and decided on abdication, and compelled Maximian to follow suit. On 1 May AD 305, on a parade ground outside of Nicomedia, the frail and emotional emperor announced his abdication to the army. Galerius was promoted to the rank of Augustus in the East.

Maximinus. Galerius hoped his nephew would be easy to control as Caesar, but he was independent and ambitious. (RHC Archive)

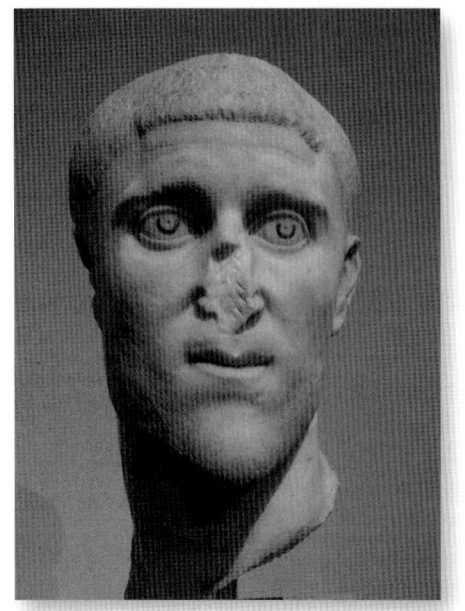

Constantius I, the father of Constantine. He reigned for little more than a year as senior Augustus. (Capillon)

In a simultaneous ceremony in Mediolanum (Milan), Maximian abdicated and Constantius was elevated to Augustus in the West and, on account of his age, became the senior emperor in the imperial college.

Constantine stood on the tribunal with Diocletian and Galerius at Nicomedia and, along with the troops witnessing this unprecedented event, anticipated his promotion to Caesar. But they were to be disappointed. Galerius disliked Constantine and wished to consolidate his hold on the imperial college by the promotion of his nephew, Maximinus Daia, to Caesar of the East. It was Galerius' hope that Candidianus, his young son by a concubine, would eventually succeed him, but until that ambition could be realized, Maximinus would act as his puppet.

Galerius was a huge and fearsome warrior and more than capable of intimidating others, but he knew that Diocletian would not be bullied and instead worked on the old emperor's conservatism and sense of duty and order. He emphasized Constantine was too ambitious and would not respect his authority. So Constantine was overlooked in the succession in the East. Galerius also interfered in the succession in the West, ensuring that his loyal henchman Severus assumed the rank of Caesar at Mediolanum. Here the frustrated party was Maxentius, the son of Maximian. Galerius had convinced Diocletian that Maxentius was insolent and unfit to rule.

The empire was divided between the new Augusti and Caesars as follows. Constantius was content with the dioceses of Britannia, Gaul (incorporating the German provinces on the Rhine frontier) and Hispania. Severus held Italia (incorporating Raetia and Corsica and Sardinia) and Africa (the Mauretanian and Numidian provinces, Africa Proconsularis, Byzacena and Tripolitana). Galerius' realm stretched from Pannonia in the west (including Noricum and Dalmatia), through Moesia and Thracia, to Asiana and Pontica in the east. Maximinus controlled the extensive diocese of Oriens, taking in the sensitive frontier with the Persian Empire and stretching across North Africa to the border with Tripolitana.

AUGUSTUS AND *PRINCEPS*

Constantius I would reign for little more than a year. Perhaps it was the lingering effects of the wound he had sustained in the rout of the Alamanni at Lingonica (Langres) in AD 302 or campaigning on the frozen Rhine in the winter of AD 304. Whatever the cause, the gods were calling him and the emperor knew death was near. In the summer of AD 305, he summoned Constantine from the East to join him on a campaign against the Picts in Britain. Dissatisfied with the succession settlement, the ailing Augustus intended to introduce Constantine to the soldiers of the West as his preferred heir.

Constantius died at Eburacum (York) on 25 July AD 306. Constantine, conspicuous from his service in the victorious campaign against the Picts, was presented to the army and proclaimed emperor. Not as the Caesar, and ultimately successor to Severus as Constantius had probably intended, but as Augustus. Galerius, now the senior emperor, was initially incensed by this usurpation. He refused to recognize Constantine as Augustus but acquiesced in his elevation to Caesar and so made him a legitimate member of the imperial college. Constantine was satisfied with this – for the moment.

When news of Constantine's succession reached Rome, Maxentius was furious. He raged about the injustice of how Constantine, the bastard of a concubine, had usurped him, the legitimate son of the Augustus Maximian. Constantine was, in fact, legitimate, but his mother, Helena, was of very humble origins and had married Constantius when he was a young officer in c. AD 270. This union was dissolved in the later AD 280s when Constantius, by then a successful general, was being groomed for entry into Diocletian's prospective imperial college and encouraged to marry Theodora, the daughter of Maximian. But Constantine's elevation also emboldened Maxentius to act.

Constantine as 'noble Caesar' in AD 307. Maximian invested him as Augustus in AD 308. (RHC Archive)

Maxentius was residing with his wife Galeria Maximilla (daughter of Galerius, and grand-daughter of Diocletian) and son Romulus on an estate on the Via Labicana to the east of Rome. He was comporting himself as a traditional Roman senator (*ILS* 666) and was well placed to take advantage of discontent in the capital. As senior emperor, Galerius ordered Severus to carry out a census in Italy for the assessment of tax. Southern Italy and especially Rome, on account of its ancient prestige and status as the capital of the Empire, had been exempt from taxation. The effective demotion of Rome to the status of any other city in the Empire, as much as the imposition of direct taxation, led to a disturbance on 28 October AD 312 in which Abellius, the *vicarius* (deputy) of the urban prefect was killed. The disturbance was led by the officers Marcellianus and Marcellus, and Lucianus, the overseer of the pork market where a free meat ration was distributed to the citizens. They were supported by the praetorians, horse guardsmen and soldiers of the urban cohorts who proceeded to proclaim Maxentius as *princeps* ('first citizen').

When Diocletian visited Rome in late AD 303, he decided that the city did not require such a large garrison and greatly reduced the number of praetorians and other troops based there. He presumably distributed the bulk of the praetorians and horse guardsmen between the courts of the Augusti and Caesars. Diocletian already had a force of praetorians with him in Nicomedia in February AD 303, and guardsmen, perhaps the praetorians attached to the court of Constantius, led the acclamation of Constantine at Eburacum. In AD 306, only a token number of guardsmen remained in Rome and Galerius, who preferred new bodyguard units such as the *scutarii* (shield-bearers, in which he ensured the young Maximinus was enrolled: Lact. *DMP* 19.6), decided to complete what Diocletian had started by removing these *remansores* (the remainder) and closing the praetorian camp.

7

Zosimus identifies Marcellianus and Marcellus as taxiarchs, the Greek term for a tribune or centurion (Zos. 2.9.3). They were tribunes or *praepositi* (temporary commanders) of the remainder of the Guard. It may be that one represented the praetorians and the other represented the *equites singulares Augusti*, the Imperial Horse Guards. The training ground and principal cemetery of the horsemen was at Ad Duas Lauros (Two Laurels), 5km to the east of Rome on the Via Labicana (Speidel 1994a, 114, 152–153). The public villa in which Maxentius was residing immediately before his elevation was located at the sixth milestone of the Via Labicana, and he appears to have owned a country estate farther along the road at Gabii (cf. the find-spots of *ILS* 666–667). The newly proclaimed *princeps* was probably escorted into Rome by horsemen from Ad Duas Lauros. Lucianus was also the tribune of the three Urban Cohorts. Previously, each cohort had its own tribune but, following Diocletian's reorganization of Rome's garrison, the strength of the *urbaniciani* was so diminished that all three cohorts came under the command of a single tribune, who also had responsibility for the pork market (cf. *ILS* 722).

Maxentius' elevation was supported in the south of Italy and, importantly, Africa, the principal source of Rome's grain. With his food supply secure, Maxentius sought to legitimize his regime by inviting his father Maximian to resume the purple as Augustus. The Senate concurred with the *princeps* and Maximian, an unwilling retiree in Campania or Lucania, accepted the invitation with alacrity.

LEFT
Maxentius. Disappointed by the succession of AD 305, he took advantage of discontent in Rome and was proclaimed *princeps* in AD 306. (Jebulon)

RIGHT
Maximian. A faithful comrade to Diocletian but treacherous to his own son and Constantine. (G. Dall'Orto)

When Maximian still ruled with Diocletian, Maxentius refused to do obeisance to his father. Maxentius was initially groomed to be his father's heir but Diocletian's establishment of the Tetrarchic system, that is the imperial college of two Augusti aided by two Caesars, in AD 293, pushed him down the line of succession, and Maximian's compliance with the abdication and imperial settlement scheme of Diocletian and Galerius entirely removed him from it in AD 305. There was little love lost between Maxentius and his father, but the new *princeps* realized the air of legitimacy the presence of Augustus Maximian would lend him if he came out of retirement. More importantly, Maxentius required Maximian as a figurehead to attract much-needed military support.

ITALY INVADED

If Galerius was infuriated by the elevation of Constantine, he was incandescent with rage at the usurpation of Maxentius, whom he despised. Severus, ostensibly Galerius' fellow-Augustus but in reality his lackey, was ordered to suppress Maxentius. Early in AD 307, Severus left Mediolanum with a powerful field army, including elite Mauri horsemen. Less than two years earlier, this army had been under the command of Maximian. Confronted with the daunting prospect of laying siege to symbolic Rome with its *c*.19km-long circuit of walls and uneasy about fighting against its former commander, the soldiers were induced to desert when offered bribes by Maxentius. The bulk of the army, including the praetorian prefect Anullinus, went over to Maxentius and Maximian. The few troops who remained loyal to Severus fled with him to Ravenna. Maximian followed and Severus surrendered himself after a short siege. He was promised his life on the condition that he abdicated, and was retained as a hostage to use against Galerius.

The walls of Rome. The 19km circuit was built by Aurelian in AD 271–275 and proved Maxentius' greatest defence against Severus and Galerius. (Karelj)

Maxentius was now in control of all peninsular Italy, but the north remained loyal to Galerius, and the mints at Ticinum (Pavia) and Aquileia continued to issue coins in his name. In the summer, Galerius crossed the Julian Alps and advanced into central Italy. He established a base at Interamna (Terni) on the Via Flaminia, some 100km north of Rome. Despite now having a powerful army, Maxentius was too canny to meet Galerius in the field. Galerius was a renowned general and extender of empire; in AD 298, he won a famous victory over the Persians in Armenia, devastated their empire, captured Ctesiphon and forced the king Narses to cede territories across the Tigris. More recently Galerius had defeated the Marcomanni, Carpi and Sarmatians. Maxentius sensibly withdrew behind the walls of Rome, which he had repaired and strengthened.

Galerius had apparently never before visited Rome and was overawed by the scale of the city when he finally saw it. In AD 298, the great victory over Narses had been gained after the emperor, with only two horsemen to accompany him, took on the role of *speculator* (scout) and personally reconnoitred the enemy camp (Fest. *Brev*. 25; Eutrop. 9.25). It is possible then, that Galerius first glimpsed Rome in AD 307 while leading a scouting party down the Via Flaminia. Realizing the difficulties of effectively surrounding and assaulting such a huge city, he decided instead to negotiate with Maxentius and offer him a degree of official recognition. Galerius' lieutenants Licinius and Probus were sent to Rome but Maxentius rebuffed them.

Meanwhile, Maxentius' agents had infiltrated Galerius' camp at Interamna and were working on his soldiers. What sort of justice was it, they asked, for a father-in-law to attack his son-in-law? How could Roman soldiers contemplate attacking Rome? And they presumably promised the

Galerius defeats Narses on the Arch of Galerius, Thessaloniki. Galerius was an accomplished general but faltered before the walls of Rome in AD 307. (D. Diffendale)

same financial rewards and promotions that had secured the defection of Severus' army. A significant number of legionaries deserted to Maxentius, and Galerius was forced to make an emotional appeal to prevent the remainder of his army following suit. The scale of desertions was such that Galerius was forced to evacuate Italy entirely but he allowed his troops to devastate and plunder as they retreated, which served only to reinforce the public image of Maxentius not as a usurper but as the defender of Rome and Italy. Severus, who was being held at a place called Tres Tabernae (Three Taverns) to the south of Rome, was no longer useful to Maxentius and was either executed or compelled to commit suicide on 15 September.

The victory over Galerius belonged to Maxentius alone. Maximian had been in Augusta Treverorum (Trier) negotiating an alliance with Constantine. Fausta, the daughter of Maximian, was given in marriage to Constantine, and Maximian conferred the rank of Augustus on his new son-in-law. But this bought only Constantine's neutrality and he refused to cross the Alps and attack Galerius as he retreated to Pannonia.

ALEXANDER AND LICINIUS

When Maximian returned to Rome, he found his status diminished. The expulsion of Galerius from Italy had consolidated Maxentius' position and popularity. The title of *princeps*, with its senatorial overtones and deliberate evocation of the emperor Trajan, had been abandoned and he was styling himself Augustus – presumably having been formally acclaimed with the rank by the troops. Maximian found it hard to believe that his old soldiers, the men who had defected to him from Severus, now preferred his son. He called a *contio*, an assembly of the citizens and soldiery, and blamed Maxentius, who was beside him on the platform, for the current ills of the Roman state. He then dramatically tore the imperial purple cloak from Maxentius' shoulders. This did not meet with the approval of the crowd. Maxentius leapt from the tribunal into the arms of his loyal soldiers and the baffled Maximian was chased from the city (April AD 308). He fled to the court of Constantine.

Maxentius was now sole ruler of Italy, Sicily, Corsica, Sardinia and the diocese of Africa, but Maximian remained popular in African provinces because of his successful campaigns against the Quinquegentanei (the 'Five Peoples' confederation) and other Mauri tribes in AD 297–98. Troops at Carthage (Tunis) in Africa Proconsularis mutinied, seized vessels and attempted to sail for Alexandria (Egypt formed part of Maximinus' territory). The flotilla was intercepted, presumably by the Misene fleet, and forced back to Carthage. Maxentius then demanded that Domitius Alexander, a *vicarius* of the praetorian prefect and responsible for the administration of the African diocese, hand over his son as a hostage. Alexander refused and declared himself emperor at Carthage (late spring–summer). He immediately severed Rome's grain supply, which led to shortages and severe disorder in the city. In one incident, a praetorian of Moesian origin, most likely one of the deserters from the armies of Severus or Galerius, was killed and the Guard, now returned to its full strength of almost 10,000 men, went on the rampage and slaughtered 6,000 citizens. Only Maxentius' personal intervention prevented an even greater massacre.

Meanwhile, Galerius sought the advice of Diocletian and conferred with him at Carnuntum (Petronell) in Pannonia (November AD 308). Maximian also attended the conference, evidently travelling from Gaul via Raetia, which had formed part of the domains of Severus but had not fallen to Maxentius. Galerius hoped to persuade Diocletian to resume the purple and use his prestige and authority to restore order to the unravelling imperial college. But Diocletian would not become emperor again; he wished only to return to his gardens at Salona (Split) and tend his cabbages. He did insist, however, that Maximian abdicate again and likely agreed with Galerius that Constantine be demoted to Caesar. Licinius, the loyal lieutenant who had stood by Galerius during the debacle of the Italian campaign, was made Augustus in place of Severus and charged with the suppression of Maxentius. He was given the diocese of Pannonia as his base.

The official college of four emperors, two Augusti and two Caesars, was thus re-established, but neither Constantine nor Maximinus was willing to submit to the authority of Galerius as senior Augustus. Galerius attempted to placate them with the honorific title *filii Augustorum* (sons of the Augusti), but Constantine continued to use the rank with which he had been invested by Maximian, and Maximinus, hardly the compliant stooge Galerius expected him to be, was angered by the elevation of Licinius to Augustus while he remained a mere Caesar. He was soon hailed as Augustus by his troops. Galerius conceded defeat in AD 309–10 and finally recognized Constantine and Maximinus as Augusti; the precarious Tetrarchy was now a college of four Augusti.

Licinius invaded Maxentian Italy in AD 309, but appears to have seized only the peninsula of Histria (Istria) and was either unwilling or prevented from advancing farther west (Barnes 1981, 33). The events of AD 312 suggest that Maxentius had already established strong forces at Aquileia and in the vicinity of Verona to counter any incursions by Licinius over the Julian Alps or through the Brenner Pass. A gravestone from Promona (near Knin) in Dalmatia, not far from Histria and in the territory of Licinius, commends the 50-year-old *protector* Valerius Valens to the Divine Manes. He 'was killed in the civil war in Italy', fighting for Licinius against the Maxentians in AD 309 (*ILS* 2776).

Maxentius' main military concern in AD 309 was Domitius Alexander. The former *vicarius* had not only stopped the grain supply from Africa, but a milestone from Sardinia names him as emperor and indicates that he controlled the island for a time (*AE* 1966, 169). This was potentially disastrous for Maxentius because Sardinia was another important granary for Rome. Not only was Maxentius failing to secure Rome's primary food supply, he had a large army to pay and levied a tax in gold from the citizens – the same citizens who had supported him in AD 306 because he stood against Galerius' imposition of taxation on the capital. The continuance of Maxentius' rule depended on the rapid suppression of Alexander. Rufius Volusianus, an aristocratic senator who had governed Africa Proconsularis in AD 305–6 (*ILS* 1213), was

Licinius. Galerius elevated his old comrade to Augustus in AD 308 and tasked him with the suppression of Maxentius. (RHC Archive)

made praetorian prefect (normally an equestrian post) and tasked with the recovery of the diocese. His task force was small, just 'a few cohorts' (Aur. Vict. 40.18), but probably represented the cream of the reformed Praetorian Guard and would have drawn on the expertise of those veterans who had served with Maximian in Africa in AD 297–98. As a senator, Volusianus had no experience of military command and was assigned a number of *duces* (generals) including a certain Zenas, 'a man celebrated for his military skill and gentle character' (Zos. 2.14.3). However, Zenas displayed little gentleness when he masterminded the rout of Alexander's army somewhere near Carthage. That great city was then sacked. Alexander himself escaped to Cirta (Constantine) in Numidia, but it was taken by siege, the pretender was captured and strangled, and the city was razed to the ground. Other towns and cities, such as Cillium (Kesserine), were pillaged and badly damaged in the campaign of reprisals (*ILS* 5570). Prominent supporters of Alexander were hunted down and crucified (cf. *CIL* VIII 18261) and their estates and property were confiscated.

At the close of AD 309, Maxentius was in a strong position. The utter defeat of Alexander and reconquest of Africa signalled to the other emperors that his army was well led and effective in battle; it would not be an easy task to remove him from Italy. Maxentius' popularity in Rome was certainly diminished, but the city's food supply was secure (Sardinia was also recovered: cf. *Pan. Lat.* 12(9).25.2), and the rich plunder from Africa removed the need for further exactions or taxation in the capital.

MAXIMIAN'S TREACHERY AND CONSTANTINE'S VISION

Throughout this period, the official emperors were concerned with the protection of the imperial frontiers. Galerius and Licinius waged regular campaigns against the Sarmatians and Carpi, and Constantine was frequently occupied with operations against various German tribes and confederations. In AD 310, while Constantine was campaigning against the Franks on the Rhine, Maximian (who was acting as Constantine's lieutenant in southern Gaul, and perhaps in command of an army group that was based at Arelate (Arles) to counter any hostile moves by Maxentius) declared Constantine had died and consequently resumed the rank of Augustus. However, the majority of troops at Arelate were not convinced. Those who accepted Maximian's tale, or at least the bounty he offered, followed their new leader to Massilia (Marseilles).

Constantine promptly abandoned his operation against the Franks and sped south. He paused at the sanctuary of Apollo Grannus (Grand), where he claimed to have experienced a vision of the god, promising him victory and 30 years of rule. Thereafter, Sol Invictus (the Unconquered Sun),

Constantine and his protector Sol on a medallion minted at Ticinum. AD 312–313. (Jastrow)

Inscription from Rome noting the descent of Constantius II and Constantine from Claudius Gothicus. (RHC Archive)

who was closely associated with Apollo, became Constantine's favoured deity. Belief in solar monotheism made him sympathetic to Christianity, and Sol was increasingly associated with Christ in the emperor's thinking.

Massilia surrendered after a short, but not uneventful, siege. Constantine failed to ensure that the assault ladders were long enough and his more valiant and reckless soldiers gained the battlements 'by stretching their bodies and by being lifted up on the shoulders of those below them' (*Pan. Lat.* 6(7).19.6). Maximian was severely reproached for his treachery but nonetheless pardoned. Following a subsequent plot to murder Constantine while he slept (perhaps actually the invention of Constantine's propagandists), Maximian conveniently committed suicide. He did so by the most disgraceful method: hanging.

Constantine proceeded to disassociate himself from the tainted memory of Maximian. Both he and his father had received the rank of Augustus from Maximian, but Constantine now revealed to his subjects a secret of huge import. He was in fact related by blood to Claudius II (r. AD 268–70), the great emperor who won the title Gothicus for his destruction of the marauding Goths. This fiction was probably suggested to Constantine because of Claudius' association with the battle of Naissus (Nish), the scene of a great defeat of the Goths in AD 269, and also the place of Constantine's birth in AD 272–73. Constantine's right to rule was established by his descent from Claudius II, and confirmed by the Sun God and force of arms.

THE DEATH OF GALERIUS

Galerius died in April 311. He had been incapacitated for some time by a horrible illness that 'devoured his genitals' (*Epit.* 40.4), probably a cancer, and Licinius had been increasingly occupied with taking over the senior emperor's duties on the Danube frontier. Galerius was an ardent pagan and had been the most enthusiastic persecutor of the Christians but, as his dealings with Constantine and Maximinus reveal, his initial rage was usually followed by a pragmatic approach. He conceded the failure of the official and brutal campaign against the Christians and issued an edict of toleration from his deathbed. As soon as the penitent senior Augustus had expired, Maximinus and Licinius raced to secure his domains. Maximinus seized Asia Minor and Licinius expanded his realm from the borders of Italy to the Black Sea. The armies of Licinius and Maximinus massed on either side of the Bosporus but the emperors met on a ship in the straits and agreed, for the time being, to be content with their current gains.

It was Constantine's ambition to reunite the empire under his sole rule (Eutrop. 10.5). His self-confident elevation as Augustus in AD 306 suggests this was his intention from the very beginning and the vision of Apollo at Grand merely provided divine assent, but the opportunity to start the process presented itself only when the original Tetrarchs – Diocletian, Maximian and Galerius – were either definitely retired or dead. In AD 311 then, Constantine brokered an alliance with Licinius, which was sealed by the betrothal of his sister, Constantia, to Licinius. Maximinus and Maxentius were obviously concerned about this. A diplomatic channel was opened between them, and Maximinus, now technically the senior Augustus, gave Maxentius the official recognition he craved. Maxentius' propaganda now rehabilitated Maximian; Constantine was a murderer and Maxentius would forcibly avenge his father. This was effectively a declaration of war, but Maxentius made no attempt to attack Constantine, who was preoccupied with a reorganization of the defences of the Rhine frontier. Maxentius continued to view Licinius, who had been assigned Italy by the conference of Carnuntum, as his most pressing threat. The cold war between Licinius and Maximinus was heating up and might at any time erupt into open conflict, but Maxentius could not rely on Licinius' attention being permanently diverted away from the prize of Italy and his defensive strategy remained centred on the maintenance of large forces in the north-east.

Constantine's activity on the Rhine frontier suggested to his fellow-emperors that he was preparing for a major campaign against the Germans. They were quite wrong. He was quietly mustering a field army for the invasion of Italy in the spring of AD 312.

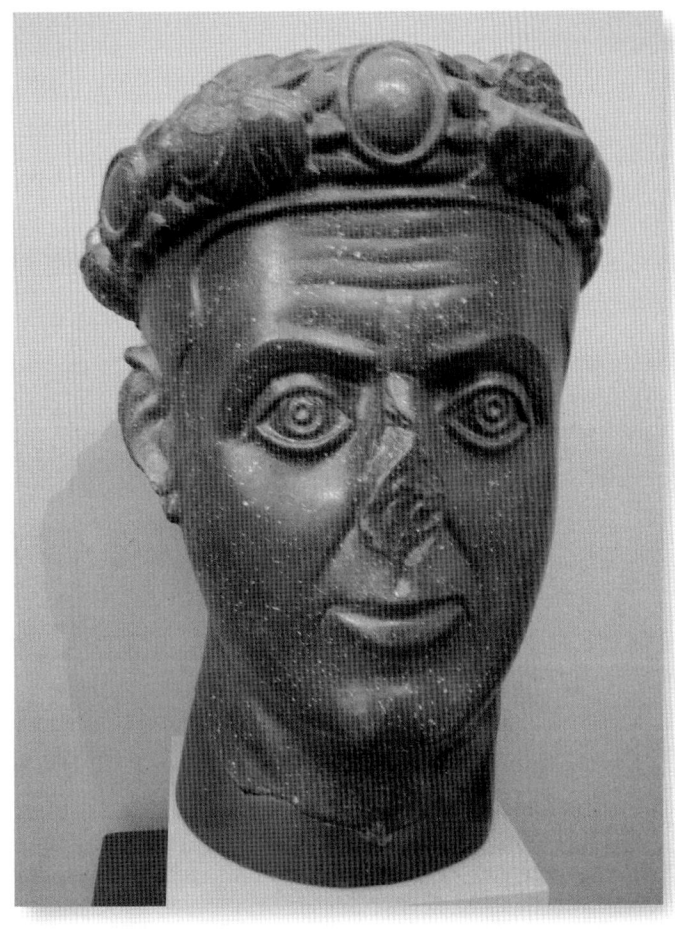

Late portrait of Galerius. When he died in AD 311 the imperial college was in crisis and civil war was brewing. (D. Entwistle)

CHRONOLOGY

306 — Death of Constantius at Eburacum (25 July); his army hails Constantine as Augustus. Galerius recognizes Constantine only as Caesar and Severus succeeds as Augustus in the West. Discord in Rome over Galerius' intention to tax the populace and remove the remainder of the praetorian cohorts; Maxentius is elevated during a disturbance against the *vicarius* of the urban prefect (28 October). Maxentius becomes *princeps* and invites Maximian to resume rank of Augustus

307 — Galerius instructs Severus to remove Maxentius. He advances on Rome but his army deserts to Maximian. Severus flees to Ravenna, which is besieged by Maximian; Severus surrenders and abdicates (spring). Galerius invades Italy and reaches Interamna but retreats when parts of his army desert to Maxentius (late summer). Execution or suicide of Severus at Tres Tabernae (15 September). Maximian concludes alliance with Constantine, elevating him to Augustus

308 — Maximian fails to depose Maxentius and flees to Constantine's court (April). Domitius Alexander revolts against Maxentius in Africa, seizes Sardinia and cuts off Rome's grain supply (summer–autumn). Galerius confers with Diocletian at Carnuntum (11 November): Diocletian declines Galerius' request to resume power; Maximian, also present, is compelled to abdicate again; Licinius, a comrade of Galerius, is made Augustus in place of Severus and tasked with the defeat of Maxentius. Dissatisfaction of Constantine and Maximinus who remain Caesars in the official imperial college

308–9 — Food shortages and disturbances in Rome. Maxentius collects a tax in gold; fighting between the populace and the Praetorian Guard

309 — Licinius seizes Histria from Maxentius. Rufius Volusianus and Zenas defeat Alexander and reconquer Africa for Maxentius (autumn–winter)

310 — Maximian rebels against Constantine and seizes Massilia. Constantine abandons campaign against the Franks to confront Maximian (July); he experiences vision of Apollo at Grand and then recaptures Massilia. Maximian is pardoned but later commits suicide after apparently attempting to assassinate Constantine

311 — Galerius issues edict of toleration for Christians and then dies (April–May); Licinius and Maximinus scramble to seize Galerius' territories. Alliance between Constantine and Licinius; Maximinus recognizes Maxentius. Death of Diocletian (3 December)

312 — Constantine invades Italy via the Cottian Alps. He captures Segusio, and defeats Maxentian armies at Augusta Taurinorum, Brixia and Verona; Aquileia and Mutina are taken by siege (spring–summer). Constantine advances on Rome by the Via Flaminia (late summer–autumn). Possible Maxentian success against Constantine's vanguard at Saxa Rubra (c.26 October); Constantine camps in the region of the Milvian Bridge, where he is instructed in a dream to mark the sign of the Christian god on his soldiers' shields (night of 27–28 October); Maxentius meets Constantine in battle at Tor di Quinto but is defeated and drowns while attempting to cross the Tiber (28 October). Constantine enters Rome in triumph (29 October)

OPPOSING FORCES

CONSTANTINE'S ARMY

In AD 312, Constantine's territory comprised the British, German, Gallic and Spanish provinces. If the anonymous panegyrist of AD 313 is correct, the combined garrisons (military and probably also naval) of these regions amounted to something approaching 160,000 men. After a careful reorganization of the defences of the turbulent Rhine frontier, Constantine selected somewhat less than 40,000 men for the field army that would invade Italy (*Pan. Lat.* 12(9).2.6, 3.3, 5.1 2).

Constantine's army was divided into four main categories: guardsmen and others attached to his *comitatus* (court); legions; cavalry *vexillationes* and infantry *auxilia*; and old-style auxiliaries (*cohortes* and *alae*).

Constantine's guardsmen with their praetorian standards. Column base on the Arch of Constantine. (RHC Archive)

Guardsmen

Constantine inherited his father's army, which included the guardsmen who acclaimed him as emperor at Eburacum (Zos. 2.9.1). As we have seen, new imperial guards units like the *scutarii* had appeared, but in AD 306 the Praetorian Guard retained its seniority in the hierarchy of the Roman army. As Caesar and senior Augustus, Constantius I had a substantial number of praetorians (and *equites singulares Augusti*) attached to his court. When Constantine invaded Italy in AD 312, he probably no longer called these guardsmen praetorians. For 500 years, since the era of Scipio Africanus, this proud moniker had identified the bravest men chosen to guard the *praetorium*, the tent of the general (Festus 223L–M), but it had been tainted by the proclamation of Maxentius as *princeps* by praetorian *remansores* in Rome. But Constantine's guardsmen still marched into battle beneath classic praetorian *signa* (standards) bearing the eagle of Rome, *imago* (portrait) of the emperor and *corona* (crown) of valour. These *signa* can still be seen on a column base on the Arch of Constantine (Speidel 1987, 378).

With their headquarters in the Castra Praetoria at Rome, the ten cohorts of praetorians, each optimally of 960 men (composed of six double-strength centuries of 160), formed the largest military force at the immediate disposal of the emperor. From the reign of Septimius Severus (AD 193–211), the Guard had formed the core of imperial field armies. It also sent out detachments of *stationarii* across the empire: to guard important ports concerned with the supply of grain to Rome (e.g. Rusicade: *ILS* 9073, AD 268–70); to police major mercantile cities (e.g. Smyrna: *IK* XXIII 382) or centres of imperial administration (e.g. Ephesus: *ILS* 2051); and to patrol strategic highways and hunt down bandits (cf. Dio 76.10.6; *ILS* 509). These roles continued into the AD 280s.

When Maximian campaigned against the Bagaudae in AD 285, he was accompanied by praetorians. One of his cohorts was then attached to a force based at Bononia (Boulogne) and tasked with clearing the coast of Frankish and Saxon pirates; this cohort supported the usurpation of Carausius, a highly successful commander who generously distributed plunder to his men, in the following year (Eutrop. 9.21 and *RIC* V² Carausius 12; Casey 1994, 92).

In AD 280–81, Aurelius Martinus, a cavalryman of the seventh praetorian cohort, was a *stationarius* at Maionia in Lydia, where he fulfilled a vow by making a dedication to Olympian Zeus (*AE* 2001, 1871). Martinus' dedication illustrates how the cavalry element of the praetorians was integrated within the cohorts. In fact, the cavalrymen remained on the rolls of the infantry centuries in which they originally enlisted (e.g. *ILS* 2054). However, a little over a decade later, in the first year of the Tetrarchy, the bulk of the cavalry element of the praetorians had been hived off to create the *equites promoti dominorum nostrorum*, the 'promoted cavalry of our lords' (*P.Lond.* III 731; Hoffmann 1969, 243–246).

After campaigning with Galerius against rebels in Egypt in AD 293–95, these cavalrymen did not return to their parent cohorts but instead remained with the emperor. The *equites promoti* are next found attached to the court of Maximinus (Lact. *DMP* 40.5) and later in the 4th century AD were organized as the *equites promoti seniores* of the elite *vexillationes palatinae*, the most senior cavalry units of the field armies, in the eastern empire (Not. Dig. Or. 5.28). There was a corresponding *vexillatio* in the western empire (Not. Dig. Oc. 6.44), which can be identified as the descendant of the praetorian *equites promoti* who served Maximian and Constantius (Speidel 1987).

Complete cohorts or large detachments of praetorians were attached to the courts of the four emperors from AD 293 and accompanied them on campaign or were deployed on internal security missions. The Guard, under the command of its prefect Asclepiodotus, played a major role in the reconquest

Saturninus and Dizala, 3rd-century horsemen of the Praetorian Guard and *equites singulares*. Diocletian removed the praetorian horse to create the *promoti* and drew on the *singulares* to establish the *comites*. (RHC Archive)

of Britannia in AD 296 (cf. Aur. Vict. 39.42) and Diocletian used the praetorians to suppress the Christians at Nicomedia in February AD 303 (Lact. *DMP* 12.5).

During his visit to Rome in AD 303, Diocletian decided that the garrison of the city was unnecessarily large and to redeploy the troops elsewhere (Aur. Vict. 39.47). The praetorians were distributed between emperors (cf. Zos. 2.9.1), perhaps equally, or perhaps in groups of two or three cohorts depending on the rank of the emperor, but the Castra Praetoria remained the official headquarters of the ten cohorts of the Praetorian Guard. The find-spots in Italy of bronze diplomas issued to praetorian veterans in AD 304 and 306 (*CIL* XVI 157, *AE* 1961, 240) suggest the continuity of the practice of the 3rd century AD of guardsmen returning to Rome to see out their final year or so of service while the Guard campaigned elsewhere (Hdn. 7.11.2). When Galerius announced his intention in AD 305–6 to close the Castra Praetoria (Lact. *DMP* 26.3), he signalled not only the end of this practice but the effective dissolution of the Guard itself and that the praetorian cohorts or detachments at the imperial courts would, like the *equites promoti*, become independent units.

The *equites singulares Augusti*, comprising two *numeri* (units) each 1,000 strong, retained its bases in the Castra Priora and Castra Nova (Old or First and New Forts) in Rome but, like the Praetorian Guard, the Horse Guard was stripped of detachments, which were organized into the *comites Augustorum nostrorum*, 'companions of our Augusti', and, like the praetorian *promoti*, they were retained in the Tetrarchic courts (Speidel 1986, 1987). The *equites comites* who fought with Galerius in Egypt in AD 295 (*P.Oxy.* I 43r) did not return to Rome; they appear next at the court of Maximinus and would become the *comites seniores* of the *vexillationes palatinae* of the eastern empire (Lact. *DMP* 38.5; Not. Dig. *Or.* 6.28). There was a corresponding *vexillatio palatina* in the west that, along with the *promoti*, was noted for its prowess in battle (Not. Dig. *Oc.* 6.43; Amm. Marc. 15.4.10). After AD 303, there remained in Rome *pauci milites*, only a few soldiers

Galerius and his guardsmen on the Arch of Galerius. (G. Churchard)

(Lact. *DMP* 26.3), but some of these represented the original *numeri* of the *equites singulares* (Aur. Vict. 40.5; Speidel 1986, 256–257).

In AD 312, then, Constantine would have had approximately a quarter of the strength of the praetorian infantry cohorts (although he had probably ceased to refer to them as praetorians, see above) and *equites promoti*, and *c*.500 *equites comites*. To this should be added a number of other guardsmen.

As we have seen, new guards units were already being formed at the close of the 3rd century AD. Maximinus Daia began his military service in the *scutarii*. These shield-bearers evolved into the *scutarii* regiments of the *scholae*, each of 500 men, in the eastern empire. Another eastern *schola*, the *Gentiles* ('Foreigners'), had its origins in the Tetrarchic period (Jones 1964, 613). It seems to have been recruited by Galerius from barbarian prisoners of war in AD 303 and was subsequently attached to the court of Maximinus (Lact. *DMP* 38.6). The *scholae* later recorded in the western empire – *Scutarii*, *Gentiles* and *Armaturae* – will have had their origins in the units formed by Constantius and Constantine to supplement the guardsmen from Rome. The *Armaturae* (matched by a unit of the imperial guard in the east) were presumably drawn from the under-officers of the same name who were expert instructors of the *armatura*, a weapons drill, which, according to Vegetius, enabled those who mastered it to outfight any opponent (Veg. 1.13, 2.14). In the 3rd century AD, the *armaturae* of *legio II Adiutrix* were organized into a *collegium*, a club or association (*ILS* 2363). These organizations were also known as *scholae*, schools. Early in the 4th century AD, the *armaturae* of the Misene fleet formed a *schola* (*ILS* 5902). Being recruited from these expert fighting men, the new imperial guard regiments were appropriately called *scholae*.

Closely associated with the praetorians as *equites singulares* in the imperial field armies of the 3rd century AD were the Mauri. These North African light horsemen were feared for their hit-and-run tactics and skill with the javelin (Hdn. 6.7.8; Zos. 1.20.2). When Maximian abdicated in AD 305, his contingent of Mauri went to the Caesar Severus (Zos. 2.10.1), but some were already serving in the army of Constantius and were inherited by Constantine in AD 306. That they played an important role in the campaign of AD 312 is certain. On the Arch of Constantine, they are prominent in the friezes depicting the siege of Verona and the battle of the Milvian Bridge.

Constantine's army also included *protectores* (see The Campaign, below). The literal meaning of *protector* is bodyguard, but it identified a soldier who, usually after many years of service in the ranks, had been promoted into the junior officer class of the later empire. A corps of *protectores* was in attendance of each emperor (Lact. *DMP* 38.7) and awaited his instruction. A *protector* might be attached to the staff of a general, entrusted with a special or technical mission (intelligence gathering, inspection and restoration of civil and military installations), or given the temporary command of a regiment or detachment in the field (Trombley 1999). The most talented and favoured *protectores* became tribunes or prefects and further promotion was possible. Between AD 270 and 285, the future emperor Constantius I was *protector*, tribune and a *praeses* (regional commander) in Dalmatia, but he was unusual in being directly commissioned into the *protectores* as a young man (*Origo* 1.2). It was from the post of commander of the corps of *protectores* that Diocletian seized power in AD 284 (Aur. Vict. 39.1).

Legions

Constantine had perhaps as many as 17 legions at his disposal (Jones 1964, 59), as well as detachments originally from elsewhere in the empire, such as the *Divitenses* of *legio II Italica* (see The Campaign, below). From Britain he could call on *VI Victrix* (Sixth, Victorious), *II Augusta* (Second, Augustan) and perhaps *XX Valeria Victrix* (Twentieth, Valiant and Victorious). This last legion may, however, have been disbanded in AD 296 for its role in the revolt of Carausius (*RIC* V² Carausius 82–83; Casey 1994, 93). Spain could furnish a single but famous legion, *VII Gemina* (Seventh, Twin).

Constantine's careful reorganization of the Rhine frontier could suggest the legions of the German provinces contributing the largest contingents (*Pan. Lat.* 12(9).2.6). Following the emperor's recent German campaigns, they would certainly be the most experienced. The German legions were *XXX Ulpia Victrix* (Thirtieth, Ulpian and Victorious, Ulpius being the family name of its creator, the emperor Trajan, r. AD 98–117); *I Minervia* (First, Minervan, after Minerva, the favourite deity of its founder, Domitian, r. AD 81–96); *VIII Augusta* (Eighth, Augustan, named after the first emperor, Augustus, r. 27 BC to AD 14); and *I Martia* (First, Martian). The latter was a recent creation, being named in honour of the patron deity of Galerius; in fact, the emperor believed that he was the son of Mars (Lact. *DMP* 9.9). The legionaries of the *XXII Primigenia* (Twenty-Second, First Born) referred to themselves as the *Duoetvicensimani*, 'the men of the Twenty-Second' (*ILS* 8973 of AD 310–15). The legion was granted the supplementary titles *Constantiniana* (Constantine's Own) and *Victrix*, indicating Constantine's favour and the legion's role in one of his victories (Hanel & Verstegen 2009). *Legio VIII Augusta* was also granted the title *Constantiniana* (*AE* 2010, 1064).

Another seven legions, thought to have been created by Maximian or Constantius, may have been available to Constantine in Gaul and Germany: *XII Victrix*; *III Herculia* and a possible *IIII Iovia* (named after Hercules and Jupiter, the patron deities of Maximian and Diocletian); three legions with the title *Flavia* (Flavius being the family name of Constantius). Two other legions, the numerals of which are lost, could have been created by Constantius or Constantine: the *Dianenses* and *Solenses* (sacred to Diana and Sol, the latter being particularly important to Constantine before his conversion to Christianity).

In the early 4th century AD, old legions (i.e. units established before the accession of Diocletian) and new legions (units created by Diocletian and his co-emperors) maintained the traditional organization of ten cohorts, with six centuries of (optimally) 80 men in each cohort (*ILS* 4195; *AE* 2002, 1237). The number of cavalry in all legions was greatly increased with regular *equites* being supplemented with mounted *lanciarii* and *equites promoti* (not to be confused with the praetorian *promoti*). Two of

Lepontius, a standard-bearer of Constantine's *legio VIII Augusta*. (P. Lemaire)

Dedication by cohorts X and VII of *legio II Herculia*, one of the new Diocletianic legions, to Mithras. (RHC Archive)

Diocletian's new showpiece legions were established with complements of 6,000 men (Veg. 1.17), but the massive expansion in the number of legions, which were perhaps built around cadres of veterans from the old legions, and the formation of the new *auxilia* and *vexillationes*, resulted in a recruitment crisis that was never solved. It is likely that the legions of this era, old and new, were massively understrength.

It was no longer the practice to field complete legions in battle. In fact, the manpower of a legion could be distributed across two or more bases. It is possible that a half-legion of five cohorts might have been called up for campaign service. Half-legions were certainly used for major construction projects, such as the building of Galerius' fortified palace at Romuliana (Gamzigrad) by cohorts I–V of *legio V Macedonica* (Christodoulou 2002), but the usual practice was to send a combat vexillation (detachment, named after the *vexillum* banner the soldiers marched under) of about 400 to 1,000 legionaries (Duncan-Jones 1990).

Auxilia and Vexillationes

Legions were still considered the backbone of the Roman army, but Constantine would have drawn an equal force of infantry from the new *auxilia*. These 'assistant' units, each perhaps 600–700 men strong, were created by Maximian and Constantius from drafts of defeated and allied Germans (Jul. *Or.* 1.34C; *Pan. Lat.* 6(7).6.2; Jones 1964, 682), but after the initial German establishment, subsequent recruits were drawn from within the Empire (*AE* 1977, 806). The old auxiliary cohorts, optimally of c.500 men but probably far below that strength, were now principally concerned with frontier defence and provincial policing. The Arch of Constantine depicts soldiers wearing helmets adorned with goat-like horns. These may represent the *Cornuti*, the Horned Ones, a new *auxilium* regiment. Also likely to have been included in Constantine's field army of AD 312 was the *auxilium* of the *Regii*, the Kings, whose possible commander, the Alamannic chieftain Crocus, played a key role in Constantine's elevation at Eburacum in AD 306 (*Epit.* 41.3; Speidel 1996).

Constantine's legions included a substantial cavalry element, but his principal source of horsemen was from the *vexillationes*. The title *vexillatio* indicates that these new cavalry units, first attested in the later 3rd century AD, had their origins in detachments permanently withdrawn from other regiments. They ranked in seniority with the legions (their veterans receiving the same privileges, *AE* 1937, 232). In previous centuries, proud auxiliary *alae*, each of 500–1,000 troopers, would have provided the bulk of cavalry in an imperial field army but, along with the auxiliary cohorts, the *alae* had been effectively relegated to the status of frontier guards and they were considered inferior in rank to the legions and *vexillationes* (*Pan. Lat.* 9(4).18.2; *Cod. Just.* 55(54).3).

Commanders

Guards units, *auxilia* and *vexillationes* were commanded by *tribuni* (tribunes) or *praepositi* ('those set over'). Overall command of a legion was entrusted to a *praefectus* (prefect), but half-legions and vexillations were commanded by *praepositi*. Senior tribunes and *duces* (generals) accompanied Constantine in the invasion of Italy and were presumably given charge of divisions of the army (*Pan. Lat.* 12(9).10.3). Unfortunately, none of these senior officers is identified. The emperor's praetorian prefect was also present (*ibid*. 12(9).11.4) but, unlike Ruricius Pompeianus, Maxentius' fighting prefect, he may have been concerned more with logistics than leading guardsmen in battle (Jones 1964, 101).

MAXENTIUS' ARMY

Klaudius Ingenuus, *centenarius* of a *vexillatio* of cataphracts in the army of Constantine. (A. Fafournoux)

Remansores

When Constantine crossed the Alps in AD 312, Maxentius had about 100,000 troops to defend his Italian and African empire (*Pan. Lat.* 12(9).3.3). This was a massive increase in the meagre forces available to him on his elevation in October AD 306. His initial support came from the *remansores* of the ten cohorts of the Praetorian Guard and the two *numeri* of the *equites singulares Augusti* (above), and the much-diminished Urban Cohorts, the militarized police force of Rome (Aur. Vict. 39.47, 40.5, where *vulgus* means the Urban Cohorts: Speidel 1986, 257).

The three cohorts of the *urbaniciani* had been unusually large, each of 1,500 men and commanded by a tribune (Dio 55.24.6, probably rounded up from 1,440, i.e., six triple-size centuries of 240 in each cohort). However, following Diocletian's reduction of the garrison of Rome, a single tribune was put in charge of all three cohorts (*ILS* 722). It can be assumed that they had lost two-thirds, if not more, of their manpower.

Southern Italy declared for Maxentius shortly after his elevation. He thus secured control of the fleet at Misenum (Miseno). In the later 1st century AD, the fleet had perhaps 80 warships and other vessels, and more than 10,000 sailors and marines (*classiarii*), but much of its manpower was diverted into land operations in the 3rd century AD and Maxentius was presented with a much-diminished force (Starr 1960, 16–17, 196–197). Control of the smaller Adriatic fleet followed when Maximian captured Ravenna. The limitations of Maxentius' naval power are indicated by Domitius Alexander's seizure of Sardinia, but Constantine's blockade of Italian ports in AD 312 was apparently not successful (*Pan. Lat.* 12(9).25.2, 16.1).

When the diocese of Africa declared for Maxentius, he gained another urban cohort (*cohors I Urbana*, based at Carthage), the old *legio III Augusta*, and perhaps seven new legions that may have been established by Maximian in the aftermath of his war against the Mauri tribes. Africa also provided cavalry *vexillationes*, old-style auxiliaries and access to the Mauri recruiting grounds (Jones 1964, 59).

Deserters and praetorians

As we have seen, the army of Severus deserted in almost its entirety to Maximian and Maxentius in spring AD 307 (*Pan. Lat.* 12(9)3.4; Lact. *DMP* 26.8). The first troops to go over were the Mauri, almost certainly led by the veterans who felt a personal bond with Maximian (Zos. 2.10.1). Severus' field army would also have included guardsmen, *vexillationes* (or *numeri* that ranked as such), and legionary detachments from the north Italian garrison cities like Concordia and Aquileia. Even more legionaries deserted to Maxentius from the field army of Galerius (Lact. *DMP* 27.3). Maxentius used these legionaries to rebuild the strength of the Praetorian Guard.

Valerius Ursianus was born in Aquileia. In AD 302, he enlisted as a *probitus* (probationer) in *legio X Gemina* at the age of 18. This famous legion, called the Twin because it had been formed by the amalgamation of the remnants of Julius Caesar's renowned Tenth Legion with another unit after the battle of Actium (31 BC), had its headquarters at Vindobona (Vienna) in Pannonia in the territory of Galerius, but Ursianus probably joined the legion in his home town, which acted as one of Maximian's principal military bases and housed a number of legionary detachments, including one from *X Gemina*. In AD 307, Ursianus marched on Rome with the emperor Severus but deserted to his old commander and was rewarded with transfer to the fourth cohort of the Praetorian Guard. He died four years later (*CIL* VI 37207). Valerius Tertius was probably also Italian, recruited into a Moesian legion, perhaps the detachment of *legio XI Claudia* (Eleventh, Claudian) based at Aquileia. After five years in the legion, he was transferred to the *lanciarii*, an elite detachment of legionary specialists attached to the court of Maximian. He had been a *lanciarius* for 11 years when he deserted to Maximian and Maxentius and entered the tenth praetorian cohort (*ILS* 2045).

A possible legionary deserter from the field army of Galerius was Aurelius Bitus, who had served 14 years as a lowly *munifex* in *legio I Italica* (First, Italian). *Munifices* had to perform menial duties (*munera*), but when he transferred to the sixth praetorian cohort, Bitus was selected (*factus*) to become an *eques*; cavalrymen ranked as *immunes* – immune from carrying out fatigues (*ILS* 2055; see *ILS* 2041 and *CIL* VI 2758 for two other possible deserters from Galerius' legions who were rewarded by admission into Maxentius' Praetorian Guard).

In the latter part of his reign, Maxentius would conscript heavily in Africa and Italy (Lact. *DMP* 44.2; Adams & Brennan 1990), and raw Italian conscripts proved unwilling fighters at the battle of the Milvian Bridge (Zos. 2.16.3). In AD 306–7, however, when Maxentius was at the height of his popularity as the defender of Italy against Severus and Galerius, Italians were keen to volunteer to serve in his army, especially in the more prestigious and

Maxentius awarded the titles Roman Palatina to his Praetorian Guard (left), reviving an occasional honorific of the 3rd century AD (right). (RHC Archive)

highly paid guards and specialist units. At the age of 23, Valerius Ursinus, whose origin is given as *natione Italus*, enrolled in one of Maxentius' praetorian cohorts and became a *lanciarius*, a specialist with the *lancia* javelin (*CIL* VI 2787). The legions also contained substantial numbers of *lanciarii*, both infantry and cavalry (*P.Beatty. Panop.* 2.226ff; *AE* 1981, 777), and there existed detachments or *numeri* of *lanciarii*, such as that in which Valerius Tertius served, which were considered senior to the legions but ranked below the Praetorian Guard (cf. *ILS* 2781–2; *AE* 2010, 1246). Maxentius probably had his own unit or units of *lanciarii*. The gravestone from Rome of the aptly named Valerius Maxentius, *eques* of a *numerus lanciariorum*, dates to the start of the 4th century AD. It is even possible that Valerius, who served for six years, was an immediate Roman recruit to the army of the new *princeps* in AD 306 and was killed at the battle of the Milvian Bridge in AD 312 (*ILS* 2791).

Maxentius honoured his ten praetorian cohorts with the titles *Romana Palatina*, emphasizing the role of the Guard as the defender of Rome and its emperor in the palace on the Palatine Hill (*AE* 1934, 157). He did not restore the praetorian horse to the cohorts but instead formed a regiment of *equites promoti dominici* (*AE* 1946, 127; Speidel 1992a, 385–389). The two *numeri* of the *equites singulares* were brought up to strength and they were designated *comites* (*ILS* 9075; Speidel 1987, 377–378).

Like the other emperors, Maxentius had a corps of *protectores* (*AE* 1946, 127; the damaged *CIL* VI 32946 refers either to a *protector* or an *eques promotus* 'of our lord Maxentius Augustus').

Legio II Parthica

It is unlikely that any part of *legio II Parthica* (Second, Parthian) remained in Italy in AD 306. No mention of this famous legion occurs in the sources concerning the elevation of Maxentius.

The legion was raised by Septimius Severus soon after AD 193 and he built a fortress for it at Alba (Albano), just to the south of Rome. In the first half of the 3rd century AD, *II Parthica* was very much the personal legion of the emperors and was to be found at the core of the imperial field armies with the Praetorian Guard, *equites singulares* and Mauri, but in the second half it was deployed as vexillations and the bond with the Castra Albana was gradually broken (e.g. *AE* 1934, 193).

Epigraphic evidence for the legion in Italy is abundant until the mid-3rd century AD, after which it peters out. The legion might have maintained its headquarters at the Castra Albana until the mid-AD 280s. The tombstone at Albano of Aurelius Iulianus, who had served in the legion for 33 years, may preserve the honorific title *Aureliana*, granted by the emperor Aurelian, who reigned AD 270–75 (*AE* 1975, 171), and a vexillation of *II Parthica* appears to have defected from Maximian to Carausius in AD 286 (*RIC* V² Carausius 60–65). The legion reappears in Mesopotamia. Part of it was destroyed when Shapur II stormed Bezabde in AD 360 (Amm. Marc. 20.7.1), and it is later recorded as being based at Cepha on the Tigris (Not. Dig. *Or.* 36.30). The transfer of the legion from Italy to Mesopotamia may be connected with Galerius' Persian War (AD 298). The Castra Albana was certainly abandoned when, shortly after AD 312, Constantine granted the land on which it stood to the Church (*Lib. Pont.* 34.30).

While still based in Italy, *II Parthica* sent out detachments of *stationarii* to the highlands of Samnium (*ILS* 9087). Under Maxentius, this role was performed by legionaries who had defected from Severus or Galerius. Valerius Dizon, whose name indicates his Thracian descent, was a centurion of the Moesian *legio IIII Flavia* (Fourth, Flavian, after Flavius, the family name of the emperor Vespasian). He probably deserted from the field army of Galerius in the late summer of AD 307 and died sometime later at Venafrum (Venafro), presumably in charge of a detachment of *stationarii* (*CIL* X 4874; Seston 1980, 491).

Aurelius Mucianus, *lanciarius* of *legio II Parthica*. The legion had probably left Italy before the elevation of Maxentius in AD 306. (B. Gagnon)

Lucianus, Abitus and Vincentius, praetorians of the 3rd century AD. Note the weighted *pila* carried by Lucianus and Abitus, the characteristic weapon of the praetorian infantryman. (Steven D. P. Richardson/RHC Archive)

Legionaries of the vexillation of *XI Claudia* based at Aquileia. Note the typical armament of two javelins, cut-and-thrust sword and oval shield. (P. Lemaire)

TACTICAL ORGANIZATION

Maxentius' praetorians, and probably those Constantinian guardsmen who were originally praetorians, fought in the traditional Roman manner: after advancing into range (*concursus*), they would hurl heavy javelins (*pila*) at close range, then charge at the run (*impetus*), barge into the enemy with their shields and then hack and stab with their swords at close quarters. Some praetorians, however, specialized in the use of the light *lancia* javelin and probably employed hit-and-run tactics on the battlefield, or provided 'missile support' for their traditionally equipped comrades.

Valerius Aulucentius, a *centurio ordinarius* of *legio XI Claudia* at Aquileia. (P. Lemaire)

Some legionaries continued to use the *pilum*, or similar heavy javelins with long iron shanks, before charging to close quarters with the sword, but a substantial number in every legion were specialist *lanciarii*, while others bombarded the enemy with small lead-weighted darts called *plumbatae* or *martiobarbuli* (Mars barbs), or fought as spearmen.

Praetorians and legionaries were organized into tactical subunits called *centuriae* (centuries) of 160 and 80 men respectively. Each century was led by a *centurio* (centurion) or *ordinarius* (senior centurion in the legions), assisted by a *signifer* (standard-bearer), *optio* (centurion's deputy), *tesserarius* (officer of the watchword), *cornicen* (horn-player) and *tubicen* (trumpeter). The centurion stood in the centre of the front rank and led by example. If he fell, the *optio* took command. The signifer's standard showed the direction of attack and acted as rallying point. The *tesserarius* maintained order and prevented soldiers from falling out of rank. The musicians relayed the signals from the general or *praepositus* to the centurion and *signifer*.

There were six centuries in a legionary cohort, each commanded by a centurion with the following titles (ranked according to seniority):

pilus prior
pilus posterior
princeps prior
princeps posterior
hastatus prior
hastatus posterior

These titles harked back to the manipular legions of the 3rd and 2nd centuries BC. In the manipular legion, ten maniples of *hastati* ('spearmen') formed the first battle line, another ten maniples of *principes* ('best men') formed the second line, and a final ten maniples of *triarii* ('third-line men') made up the final line of a *triplex acies* (triple battle line). When the 30 maniples of the legion were grouped into ten cohorts at the end of the 2nd century BC, the maniple was split into two centuries, and so each cohort had two centuries of *hastati*, two of *principes*, and two of *pili* ('javelin men', another title for the *triarii*). The paired centuries were designated *prior* ('front' or 'first') and *posterior* ('rear' or 'following'). The title *posterior* suggests it formed up behind the *prior*, but in his account of the Sabis (57 BC), Julius Caesar states that he ordered the 'maniples' to open up so the legionaries had room to wield their swords effectively (*Caes. BG* 2.25). If Caesar used maniple to refer to paired centuries, it suggests *priores* and *posteriores* could fight side by side. In Caesar's day, the *triplex acies* was formed by cohorts rather than by lines of *hastati*, *principes* and *pili*. The ten cohorts of the legions assumed a 4–3–3 formation (*Caes. BC* 1.83), but when Hadrian observed the manoeuvres of *legio III Augusta* at Lambaesis in AD 128, the centuries of *pili*, *principes* and *hastati* formed up in the old manipular battle lines (Speidel 2006, 28–45).

When Aurelius Iustinus joined the Aquileia detachment of *legio XI Claudia* at the close of the 3rd century AD, he was enrolled in the century of a *hastatus posterior* (*ILS* 2332). Dizo, a contemporary of Iustinus in *XI Claudia*, served in the 'first century' (meaning the century of the *pilus prior*) of the sixth cohort that formed part of the vexillation based at Concordia (*Pais* 442). The use of these ancient centurial titles suggests they still retained their tactical significance, allowing legionary forces to adopt an array of battle formations, form a simple single line to a checkerboard formation of three interchangeable lines. As all legionary cohorts and vexillations retained this centurial organization, they could 'snap on' to any other cohort or detachment from across the Empire (Speidel 1992b).

Command and control on the battlefield: a *cornicen* and *signifer* on the Ludovisi battle sarcophagus. (RHC Archive

Praetorian centurions were not distinguished by the titles of *pilus*, *princeps* or *hastatus*, but it is likely that the six centuries of each cohort were trained to assume various formations in the manner of their legionary counterparts.

The regular order of the infantry century was in four staggered ranks, each soldier allotted six Roman feet of space to allow him to use his weapons freely. In close order, the space was reduced to three Roman feet, and the number of ranks might be doubled to eight (Polyb. 18.30.6–10; Arr. *Ect.* 15–18). Such a formation was not necessarily defensive. The praetorians or legionaries might attack as a phalanx or form the point of the *cuneus* (wedge) in a pig's head formation.

The soldiers of the *auxilia* were armed with swords, javelins and spears and fought in essentially the same manner as the praetorians and legionaries, but the internal organization of their regiments is not so well understood. We know the rank structure of the *auxilia*: tribune in command; *primicerius* as second in command, followed by the *senator*, *ducenarius* (perhaps analogous with senior praetorian or legionary centurions), *centenarius* (perhaps equivalent to a centurion), *biarchus* (this grade included the *draconarii*, the standard-bearers named after their dragon standards, cf. *ILS* 2805, and perhaps under-officers, equivalent in rank and function to the *optio*) and *circitor* (equivalent to the *tesserarius*). The cavalry *vexillationes* and *scholae* guards units shared this rank structure.

The additional under-officer post of *exarc(h)us* is found in the *vexillationes*. It has been suggested that his title derived from ξ (*hex*), the Greek word for six, and that he was in charge of a squad of six troopers (Grosse 1920, 124–125), but late Roman cavalry formations were based on squads of ten troopers (*Maur. Strat.* 2.6). In Greek, *exarchos* means leader, and a more attractive explanation is that Latinized *exarchus* was used by the Roman army to identify

Gravestone from Aquileia of Aurelius Iustinus of *legio XI Claudia*, recording his enrolment in the century of the *hastatus posterior* (line 5). (Steven D. P. Richardson)

a file leader. The *exarchus* may be identical to the *decanus*, an under-officer in charge of ten soldiers (*AE* 1951, 30; Veg. 2.8, 13; Speidel 2000, 478).

The post of *exarchus*, and perhaps also *biarchus*, existed in the *promoti* units of the legionary cavalry (*Chrest. Mitt.* 196; *P.Col.* VII 188 at line 8). At a higher level, the tactical subunits of *promoti* were led by centurions (the size of their *centuriae* is not known), who in turn were commanded by a *praepositus* (*P.Col.* VII 188).

The organization of the regular legionary *equites* and the mounted *lanciarii* is uncertain. In the 2nd and 3rd centuries AD, the *equites* were led in battle by their *exercitatores* and *magistri*, training officers of senior centurial rank (*AE* 1965, 223; *ILS* 2333). The *numeri* of the *equites singulares* were divided into *turmae* of *c*.30 men and commanded by officers called *decuriones* (e.g. *AE* 1954, 81), but the rank of decurion did not exist in the Praetorian Guard. Like legionary *equites*, the praetorian horsemen were led by *exercitatores* (*ILS* 2089). There is no evidence for *centuria* or *turma*-sized tactical subunits in the praetorian horse but *exarchi* were to be found in the ranks of Maxentius' *promoti dominici* (*AE* 1946, 127).

Cavalrymen employed a broad variety of weapons, ranging from the heavy lance (*contus*) to the light *lancia*, and bows, swords, axes, maces and clubs. The Mauri light cavalry seem not to have used any protective gear, but most cavalry were well armoured, especially horsemen classed as *catafractarii* or *clibanarii*. The difference between *catafractarii* and *clibanarii* is uncertain. It has been suggested that all heavily armoured cavalrymen were known as *catafractarii*, but *clibanarii* designated cavalry units in which both rider and horse were fully armoured (Speidel 1984). These heavy cavalrymen were principally shock troops (*Pan. Lat.* 4(10)23.4) but, like their Persian counterparts, they could also fight from a distance using bows (Jul. *Or.* 1.37D).

Relief of a cavalryman armed with an axe and a heavy infantryman in a mail coat from Galerius' palace at Gamzigrad. (A Chen/ISAWNYU)

OPPOSING COMMANDERS AND PLANS

CONSTANTINE

Flavius Valerius Constantinus, better known as Constantine, was in born in Naissus in AD 272–73 (*Origo* 2.1). Constantine's father was Flavius Constantius, the scion of a leading Dalmatian family whose high rank secured his immediate entry into the corps of the *protectores* in *c.* AD 270. Defection from Carinus to Diocletian during the civil war of AD 285 secured patronage and promotion. By AD 287, he was Maximian's right-hand man and son-in-law (Constantius had divorced Helena, the mother of Constantine), and his feats as Maximian's foremost general, and subsequently as Caesar in Germany and Britain, far outshone the victories achieved by the Augustus.

From Constantius to Constantine, the blood ran true. Constantine inherited his father's high personal courage, leadership and organizational skills. During his service as a senior tribune in the armies of Diocletian and Galerius, he emerged as a hero to rival the famous exemplars of the Roman Republic. He participated in the great defeat of Persia in AD 298 (*Oratio* 16.2), was a victor in single combat (*Pan. Lat.* 6(7).3.3), and captured a Sarmatian chieftain in battle and dragged him before Galerius (Zon. 12.33; *Origo* 2.3); wherever Constantine went, victory followed. His affability, striking appearance and commanding bearing left a lasting impression on all who met him or merely observed him from afar (Lact. *DMP* 18.10; Euseb. *VC* 1.19).

Fragments of a colossal statue of Constantine from the Basilica Nova in Rome. The basilica was built by Maxentius but Constantine adapted it to house this huge statue, which depicted the emperor holding a cross. (RHC Archive)

As emperor he remained unusually approachable, his majesty tempered by the common touch. He had a close rapport with his soldiers and was deeply concerned for the welfare of his *conveterani*, his fellow-veterans, and their families (*Cod. Theod.* 7.20.2; *Cod. Just.* 6.21.15), and this engendered in them a fierce loyalty (*Pan. Lat.* 6(7).18.1). His personal example inspired his soldiers in battle and they vied to perform valiant feats in his presence (*Pan. Lat.* 6(7).19.6). Constantine's travels and campaigns were characterized by a swiftness and energy that recalled the famous *celeritas* of Julius Caesar (*Pan. Lat.* 12(9).16.3; Lact. *DMP* 29.6), while his affinity with the divine and ability to make those around him believe that he was favoured and directed by the gods, bears comparison with Scipio Africanus.

Imbued with charisma and burning with ambition, Constantine's ultimate aim was to rule the whole empire (Eutrop. 10.5). The closer he came to achieving this, the more ruthless he became.

MAXENTIUS

The date and place of birth of Marcus Aurelius Valerius Maxentius is not known, but he was, at most, a decade younger than Constantine. He had not been born an imperial prince, but his father was elevated to the purple during his infancy; the child Maxentius was groomed in the expectation that he would succeed Maximian (*Pan. Lat.* 10(2).14.1–2). This prospect was put on hold by the promotion of Constantius and Galerius in AD 293, and again frustrated by the succession settlement of AD 305. Maxentius' anger and pride was such that he refused to bow to his father, or Galerius, at the imperial courts (Lact. *DMP* 18.9).

Like Constantine, he had served as a tribune in the army of one of the Tetrarchs, most probably Galerius, and saw some active service (Barnes 1981, 25–26). This is important, because later Constantinian propaganda went to great lengths to portray Maxentius as indolent, deviant, cowardly (cf. Aur. Vict. 40.19–20; *Epit.* 40.13), and as distinctly unmilitary (*Pan. Lat.* 12(9).14.4.). However, Maxentius did win over Maximian's veterans and they supported him when his father attempted to overthrow him in April AD 308. Later in AD 308, Maxentius was able to quell the vengeful fury of the praetorians when they rampaged through the city after the murder of one of their comrades by civilians (*Chr. Min.* I 148; Zos. 2.13). He was well liked by his soldiers and he knew how to keep them on side with forceful and persuasive harangues – a skill no doubt learned while at the courts of his father and Galerius (*Pan. Lat.* 12(9).14.6). Despite the frequent defeats they suffered in AD 312, the loyalty of Maxentius' troops did not waver; contrast the behaviour of the armies of Severus and Galerius in AD 307. That Maxentius remained in power for six years, facing the invasions of Severus and Galerius, the revolt of Domitius Alexander and the resulting civil unrest in Rome, and kept his soldiers on side throughout that time, suggests that he was a man of considerable force of personality, who was tenacious, convinced of his right to rule, and a commander-in-chief of charisma who inspired devotion until the very end (cf. *Pan. Lat.* 12(9).5.2–3, 17.1).

Maxentius Augustus. The sources are hostile to Maxentius, but he was probably a charismatic leader. (RHC Archive)

Constantine's vision of a reunited empire hinged on the liberation of Rome from Maxentius 'the tyrant'. As a symbol, Rome was hugely important. It conferred legitimacy and seniority on whoever held her. By possessing Rome, Maxentius could style himself *princeps*, pose as *conservator Urbis* (preserver of the City) and claim to be the upholder of traditional Roman morals and religion (*RIC* VI 377, no. 194, etc.; *CIL* VI 1220). Maxentius' ultimate aims are not clear. Perhaps he envisaged ruling the whole empire from Rome. He certainly intended to expand his domains. He had plans to seize Raetia, the province linking the territories of Constantine and Licinius, and use it as a base for the conquest of Dalmatia and Illyria (the Balkans) (Zos. 2.14.1). This suggests Maxentius viewed Licinius as his principal opponent; war with Constantine could wait. Of course, matters turned out very different.

THE CAMPAIGN

The following account draws on the two principal sources for the campaign, *Pan Lat.* 12(9).2–15 and 4(10).17–27.

SEGUSIO TO AUGUSTA TAURINORUM

Constantine crossed the Cottian Alps in early spring AD 312. His target was Segusio (Susa), the fortress city acting as a blockhouse on the main route to Augusta Taurinorum (Turin). Constantine's route over the Alps is not recorded, but he probably followed the main road from the garrison town of Brigantio (Briançon), over Mons Matrona (Mont Genèvre), past Ad Martis (Oulx), and down into the valley of the Duria Minor (Doria Riparia) to Segusio (Amm. Marc. 15.10.3–7). The route was notoriously difficult in winter but Constantine may have benefited from an early thaw.

The Porta Savoia at Susa, one of the original Roman gatehouses of Segusio. Constantine's engineers managed to burn their way through its mighty gates. (K. Nahr)

Maxentius was not expecting invasion by this route, at least not so early in the year, and Segusio was garrisoned by a small force of regulars and a militia of local 'Subalpine' men. The garrison was stunned by the sudden appearance of Constantine, who they believed was campaigning on the Rhine. Constantine offered to pardon the Maxentians if they opened the gates and surrendered the city to him, but they refused. Constantine immediately launched an assault on the massive walls, which were 12m high with gatehouses rising to double that height. He had learned his lesson two years before at Massilia, and the assault ladders were long enough to gain the ramparts. The defenders were bombarded with *glandes* (sling bullets) and javelins. Constantine's soldiers swarmed up the ladders and speedily dispatched the enemy with swords and spears. The emperor's engineers managed to burn through the city's gates and Segusio surrendered. The fires at the gates spread into the city, but Constantine ordered his men to douse the flames – a task that was achieved with far greater difficulty than the defeat of the garrison – and reassure the citizens that they came as liberators.

Constantine invades Italy, spring AD 312

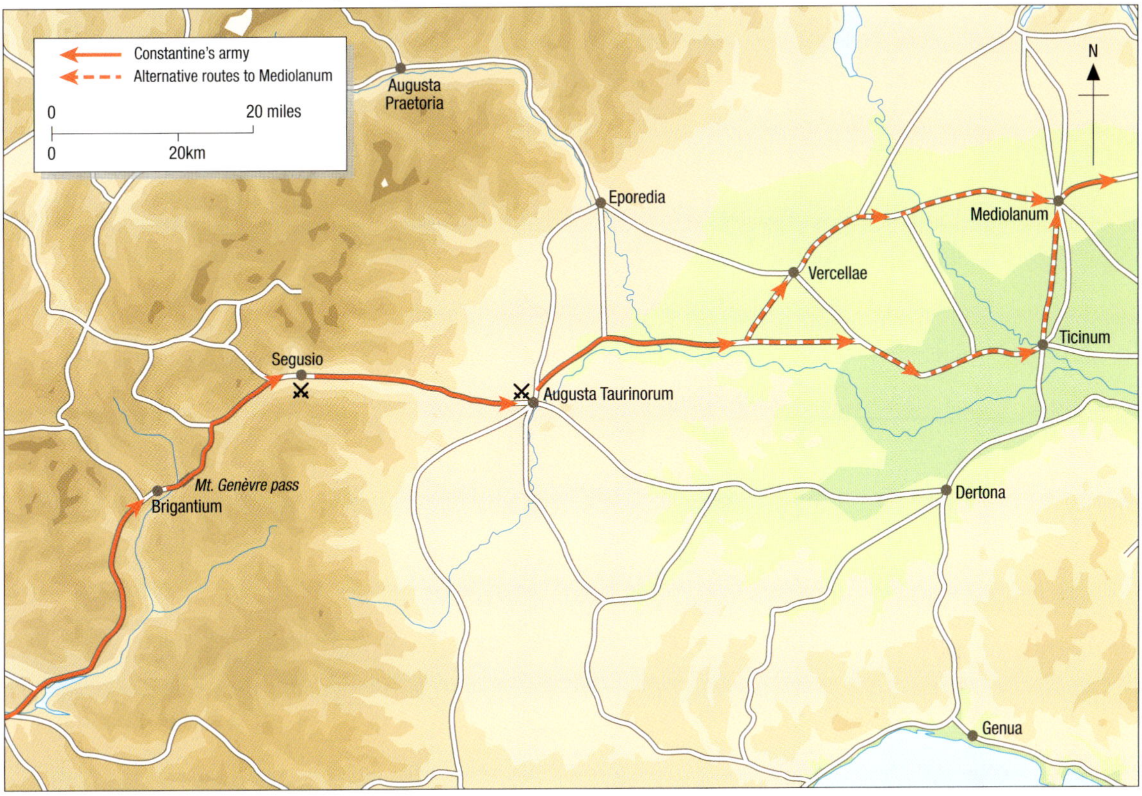

The citizens of Segusio, expecting Constantine's soldiers to go on the rampage and sack the city, were pathetically grateful to the emperor.

With Segusio captured, Constantine hastened down the valley of the Duria Minor. Maxentius and his commanders were now aware of Constantine's invasion and a field army was sent to intercept him just to the west of Augusta Taurinorum, probably in the vicinity of Rivoli (Levi 1934). The main concentration of Maxentian soldiers was far away to the east at Verona. The army that confronted Constantine must have been drawn from more local sources. Inscriptions suggest that Maxentius maintained strong garrisons at Augusta Taurinorum and Eporedia (Ivrea) to react to any incursions through the Alpine passes.

The unnamed Maxentian general had arranged his army in a *cuneus* (wedge) formation on a hill. The wings of the wedge extended behind the hill. The point of the wedge was formed by fully armoured cavalry – both rider and horse – known in Latin military slang as *clibanarii*, literally 'oven-men' (from *clibanus*, 'oven', 'furnace', also used as a

Constantine's army on the march in AD 312. The badly damaged standards held by the *signiferi* at the head of the column originally depicted Victory and Constantine's patron, Sol Invictus. Arch of Constantine. (RHC Archive)

The Porta Palatina at Turin. The citizens of Augusta Taurinorum refused to admit Maxentian fugitives, who were then massacred by Constantine's army. (Godromil)

slang term for a cuirass). The Maxentian general intended to break the centre of Constantine's army with the *clibanarii* and then swing the wings of the *cuneus* forward to envelop its flanks. But Constantine guessed what his enemy intended and organized his own battle line into a *forfex* (forceps). He took up position at the centre of the shallow V-shaped formation with his own heavy cavalry, *catafractarii*, who were trained to charge through the enemy like battering rams.

The advance of the Maxentian *clibanarii* would have unnerved other soldiers, but the *animus* (morale) of Constantine's men was high, buoyed up by their easy conquest of Segusio and by the presence of the warrior emperor in the front rank. As the Maxentians broke into a charge, Constantine and his catafracts deliberately gave ground while the wings of the army moved forwards; the *clibanarii* were unaware of the trap they had been drawn into until it was too late. Constantine then halted his retreat and attacked.

Constantine had obviously received intelligence that he would be facing *clibanarii* and equipped his soldiers with heavy clubs reinforced with iron; regular-edged weapons would have little effect on the heavily armoured troopers or their mounts. The *clibanarii* were battered from all sides. The Constantinian cavalry aimed their clubs at the riders' heads. They were so tightly packed that the dead or those who were merely stunned remained upright in their saddles. The mounts of the *clibanarii* were also clubbed, or infantrymen plunged weapons under their armoured bards. Maddened with pain, the horses were uncontrollable. The *forfex* had closed and there was no escape.

The destruction of the *clibanarii* was total. The wings of the Maxentian army did not come into play but panicked and fled. They were pursued to Augusta Taurinorum, but the citizens had barred the gates and Constantine's men embarked on a second massacre beneath the walls.

A gravestone from Eporedia (Ivrea), a little to the north of Turin, commemorates Valerius Ienuarius, a local man who served in a *vexillatio catafractariorum* (CIL V 6784). Ienuarius' *vexillatio* was a new-style unit of heavy cavalry and not a legionary detachment. His rank of *circitor* was equivalent to the legionary *tesserarius* (Veg. 3.8), the under-officer responsible for distributing the daily watchword that was essential for security in the camp and identifying comrades on the battlefield. It is thought that he was one of the Maxentian heavy cavalrymen killed in the battle.

A cluster of gravestones from Turin and Ivrea probably belong to other Maxentian casualties. Aurelius Marcianus was a cavalry *circitor* (*CIL* V 6999). The officer Aurelius Crescentianus, who bore the honorific title *vir egregius* (outstanding man), was 'killed in the battle line'; the gravestone was set up by his brother, Pistus, an *exarchus* (*CIL* V 6998). Aurelius Maximus was a 20-year-old *exarchus* of a unit of Dalmatian cavalry. He was commemorated by his friend Aurelius Victorinus, a centurion in one of the legions or Maxentius' Praetorian Guard (*ILS* 2629). Aurelius Senecio, another *exarchus* of the *numerus Dalmatarum*, survived the battle and erected a memorial for his *contubernalis* ('tent' or 'mess mate'), Aurelius Vindex (*CIL* V 7001).

The *numerus* of Maximus and Senecio also bore the title *Divitensium*, indicating that it had seen service at Divitia (Deutz), the bridgehead fort on the Rhine opposite Colonia Agrippinensis (Cologne), under Maximian in the AD 280s or 290s. The unit was later attached to Maximian's *comitatus* (court) at Milan and passed to the Caesar Severus in AD 305. It then defected from Severus to Maxentius in AD 307 (Hoffmann 1969, 258–260).

Two centurions of *legio IIII Flavia* were commemorated at Eporedia: 36-year-old Aurelius Vitalis, and a certain Marcus, whose *nomen* (family name) and age are lost (*CIL* V 6782, 6783). It is likely that they too were killed at Augusta Taurinorum, having deserted to Maxentius from the army of Galerius.

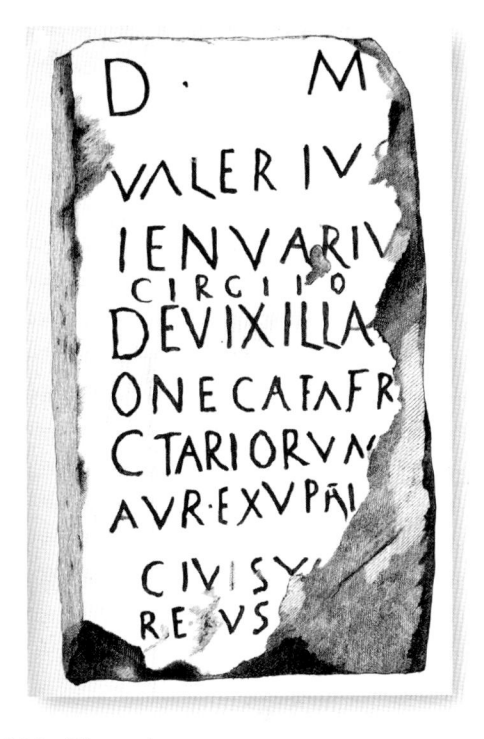

Gravestone of Valerius Ienuarius, a Maxentian *circitor* killed at Augusta Taurinorum. (RHC Archive)

Maximus, Crescentianus and Marcianus – Maxentian casualties of Augusta Taurinorum. (RHC Archive)

BRIXIA AND VERONA

Augusta Taurinorum welcomed Constantine as a liberator. Other towns and cities in the Transpadane region sent ambassadors to acknowledge him as ruler and provided supplies for his army. There was doubtless an element of pragmatism in the actions of the Transpadane settlements; those who remained loyal to Maxentius would be attacked and pillaged (cf. Zos. 2.15.1), but Constantine's invasion was probably also welcomed. Unlike privileged Rome and southern Italy, the north of Italy had been subject to taxation since the reign of Diocletian (Aur. Vict. 39.31) and the exactions necessary to maintain Maxentius' army must have fallen heavily on the north, especially on great cities like Mediolanum, which until AD 307 had been the capital of an Augustus.

Constantine's progress through the valley of the Padus (Po) seems not to have been contested. He made a triumphal entry into Mediolanum. He allowed his troops to recuperate there for some days before continuing his advance eastwards.

Constantine knew that the hardest fighting was to come. Expecting an attack from Licinius, Maxentius had concentrated his forces in and around Verona and placed them under the command of the praetorian prefect Ruricius Pompeianus, a man renowned for his tenacity and military skill. It has been suggested that his *supernomen* (nickname) was Zenas, and that he is identical with the general who defeated Domitius Alexander (Paschoud 1971, 203). He would prove to be Constantine's most dangerous opponent.

Pompeianus probably had with him detachments from the Praetorian Guard and the *equites singulares Augusti*. He sent a large force of cavalry to slow Constantine's advance from Mediolanum but it was defeated by Constantine's vanguard at Brixia (Brescia) and retreated back to Verona. The broken tombstone of an *eques singularis* has been discovered at Brixia. The iconography suggests it dates to the later 3rd or start of the 4th century AD, and it may commemorate a Maxentian casualty of the battle (Franzoni 1987, no. 49; Speidel 1994a, 153).

Constantine advanced on Verona and divided his army into two parts. The city was protected to the west, north and east by a great loop of the river Athesis (Adige). While one part of Constantine's army threatened the wall that defended the southern side of the city, the other part crossed the river (it is not clear if this was up- or downstream of the city) and secured the far bank. The city could no longer be supplied from the river.

Pompeianus attempted to break through Constantine's siege lines, but was initially forced back into Verona. Eventually, however, he did succeed in breaking out. It is not recorded how he achieved this feat, but one suspects that a

USAF aerial photo of Verona being bombed in 1944. The Roman city with its amphitheatre can be clearly seen in the central loop of the Adige. (SDASM Archives)

Constantine's conquest of Northern Italy, spring to summer AD 312

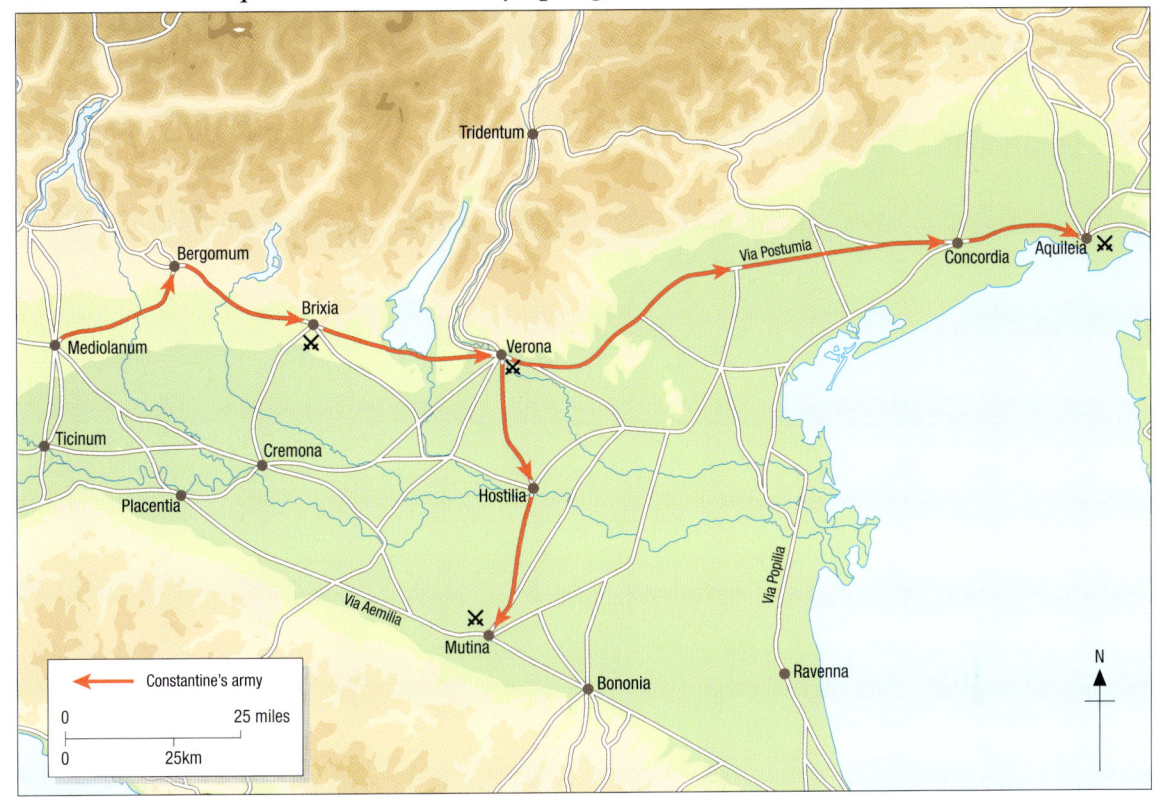

diversionary sortie, from the southern side of the city, enabled him to cross the Athesis, cut his way through the Constantinian troops on the far bank and head eastwards along the Via Postumia. It is likely that his destination was Aquileia, where Maxentius would have maintained a strong force to protect north-east Italy from incursions by Licinian forces out of Histria or over the Julian Alps.

Constantine did not pursue Pompeianus. He continued the siege of Verona, but to no avail. He clearly did not have a sophisticated siege train with him, and when Pompeianus returned with a large relief force, Constantine found himself in a precarious situation. It seemed that the besieger was about to become the besieged.

Constantine directs the siege of Verona on the Arch of Constantine. Note the Mauri bowmen at the right. (RHC Archive)

The Maxentian defenders of Verona hurl rocks and javelins at Constantine's men. (D. Entwistle)

Despite it being late in the day when the approach of Pompeianus' army was reported, Constantine decided to give battle. To prevent another breakout from Verona, he left part of the army to continue the siege. He deployed the remainder of his army (apparently the smaller part) into a *duplex acies* (double battle line), but when the large size of Pompeianus' army became evident, Constantine quickly reduced the depth of his army and formed it into a longer, single battle line (*simplex acies*) to reduce the risk of envelopment. Despite the lack of depth, Constantine believed the great *animus* of his men would prevent the Maxentians from breaking through their ranks. He was right. The soldiers were inspired by his personal example; the emperor led his cavalry from the front and slaughtered all who came before him. Yet Pompeianus and his soldiers fought on stubbornly, and the battle raged on into night. The death of the valiant Pompeianus caused the Maxentians finally to falter and Constantine accepted their surrender.

Valerius Florentius and Valerius Herodius, from Suasa in Umbria, may have died alongside Pompeianus. The brothers enlisted as guardsmen on the same day and died together, two years and six months later, while serving on the staff of a praetorian prefect (*ILS 9075*). The brothers were openly Christian, which suggests enlistment in the bodyguard of the pagan but tolerant Maxentius. They may have died on the same day as the result of an accident or epidemic, but it is tempting to see them as casualties of the epic battle at Verona (Seston 1980, 491).

Constantine was exhausted and covered in the blood of those he had slain. *Duces* (generals) and tribunes rushed to congratulate him, embracing him or grasping his hands but the emperor had little time for celebration. He returned to the siege and invited the city to surrender. The inhabitants of Verona chose to accept the emperor's clemency. The war in the north was almost over, but important cities remained to be taken. Aquileia and Mutina (Modena) were besieged, as were other strongholds. It is unfortunate that these other places are not identified by the sources.

THE ADVANCE ON ROME

The panegyrists paint Constantine's campaign as a lightning affair, his army always marching or fighting, with only a few days' respite at Mediolanum. Constantine's successes mount up in a breathless succession, but it is not known how long it actually took him to fight his way from the extreme west (Segusio) to the far east (Aquileia) of continental Italy; the siege of Verona must have lasted a number of weeks. The only securely attested dates in the whole campaign are its final days, 26–28 October. It is uncertain how much time Constantine spent securing and organizing his conquests. Perhaps he delegated such tasks to his anonymous *duces* and praetorian prefect.

When Constantine had completed his operations in Venetia (perhaps suggesting that Aquileia was the last Maxentian fortress to fall), he advanced on Rome along that most famous of roads, the Via Flaminia. Starting at Ariminum (Rimini), the road traversed the Apennines and was the most direct route to the capital. It was potentially dangerous. The Furlo Pass, known in Roman times as Intercisa or Petra, was the obvious point at which to halt Constantine's advance:

The Furlo Pass (top) and north end of the Roman tunnel (bottom) on the Via Flaminia. It was the perfect place for Maxentius to halt Constantine's march on Rome, but Constantine was allowed to pass the Apennines uncontested. (Turismo Marche)

> [The Via Flaminia] passes through extremely mountainous country… On the right of this road a river [Candigliano, a tributary of the Metaurus] descends which no man can ford because of the swiftness of the current, and on the left not far away rises a sheer rock which reaches to such a height that men who might chance to be standing on its summit, as seen by those below, resemble the size of the smallest birds. And in ancient times there was no passage through as one went forward. For the end of the rock reaches to the very stream of the river, affording no room for those who travel that way to pass by. So the men of ancient times constructed a tunnel at that point [in AD 76], and made there a gate for the southern end. And they also closed up the greatest part of the northern entrance, leaving only enough space for a small gate there also, and thus rendered the place a natural fortress, which they call by the fitting name of Petra. (Procopius, *Gothic War* 2.11.10–14)

The Aesis (Scheggia) Pass was another suitable point at which to block Constantine's army (Ashby & Fell 1921, 129), but there is nothing in the sources to suggest that Maxentius attempted to do so. However, Constantine may have encountered resistance when he reached Spoletium (Spoleto) in the heart of Umbria.

At Spoletium, a gravestone was erected for Florius Baudio, a 40-year-old veteran with 25 years' service (*ILS* 2777). His name suggests he was of Germanic origin and he died with the rank

Constantine's advance on Rome, late summer to autumn AD 312

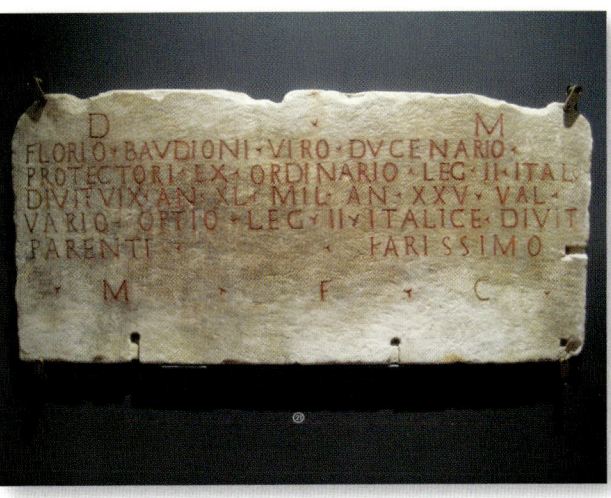

of *vir ducenarius protector*, having been promoted from the post of *ordinarius* (senior centurion) in *legio II Italica Divitensium*. The gravestone was commissioned by his son, Valerius Vario, an *optio* in the same legion. The headquarters of *legio II Italica* was Lauriacum (Enns) in Noricum. That province was in Licinius' domains but a detachment of the legion had fought in Maximian's African War in AD 297–98 and on returning to Europe it was transferred to Constantius I and quartered at Divitia and assumed the title *Divitensium*. It was thus part of the army inherited by Constantine in AD 306 (Ritterling 1924–25, 1474, 1546; Hoffmann 1969, 258–260). As a *protector*, 'bodyguard', of the emperor, Baudio was a member of the officer class of the later empire. The title of *vir ducenarius*, borrowed from the old equestrian system, indicates his seniority; he was two grades above Aurelius Crescentianus, the Maxentian *vir egregius* killed at Augusta Taurinorum (*Cod. Theod.* 12.1.5). It is possible that Baudio was the *praepositus* or *vicarius* (deputy commander) of the detachment of the *Divitenses* (compare *ILS* 546, 2784).

At Ocriculum (Otricoli), about halfway between Spoletium and Rome, two more soldiers of the *Divitenses* were commemorated. Valerius Iustinus of cohort VII was buried by his father and brother, and Valerius Saturnanus of cohort VI by his brother (*AE* 1982, 258; *CIL* XI 4085). The inscriptions do not record how the legionaries died. They may have succumbed to illness or the effects of wounds sustained in the north, but the cluster could suggest Constantine's army was attacked as it advanced down the Via Flaminia, or that Maxentian garrisons had to be removed by force from Spoletium and Ocriculum. Finally, the gravestone at Rome of Valerius Genialis, a *signifer* (standard-bearer) of the *Divitenses*, suggests that he was killed at the battle of the Milvian Bridge (*ILS* 2346). What happened at that battle will be considered next.

LEFT
Relief of a legionary from Linz, one of the bases of *II Italica*, the parent legion of the *Divitenses*. (Florian Himmler)

RIGHT
Gravestone of Florius Baudio, *ducenarius protector* and possible *praepositus* of the *Divitenses* in AD 312, at Spoleto. (Ian Ross)

THE BATTLE

PRIMARY SOURCES

There is no single satisfactory account of the battle of the Milvian Bridge. The details of the encounter and its location vary. Before attempting a reconstruction of the battle, we must survey the most important sources.

1. *The Panegyric of* AD *313*
The earliest account of the battle is found in *Latin Panegyric* 12(9).16–17, which was delivered by an elderly but unnamed orator in the presence of Constantine at Treveri (Trier) in AD 313 (cf. *Pan. Lat.* 12(9).8.1; at 9.6 the orator gently rebukes Constantine for risking his life in the fighting at Verona, perhaps suggesting familiarity with the emperor).

After describing the conquest of northern Italy, the orator states that Constantine feared Maxentius would follow his strategy of AD 307, namely that he would rather endure siege in Rome than come out and fight in open battle. By plundering the recently reconquered provinces of Africa and Sardinia, Maxentius had 'amassed provisions for an unlimited period of time' (*Pan. Lat.* 12(9).16.1).

Despite Constantine's successes in the north, the situation was not dissimilar to AD 307 when Severus and then Galerius had faltered before Rome. It seems unlikely that Constantine had an extensive siege train in his arsenal; Segusio was taken by storm, Verona surrendered only after the defeat of Ruricius, and there are no details concerning the fall of Aquileia or Mutina. We know of Constantine employing siege machines only at Byzantium in AD 324 (Zos. 2.25.1). Constantine's strategy now depended on a victory in the field. If Constantine became bogged down in a siege of Rome, Licinius may have been emboldened to attempt a second invasion of northern Italy and to extend his territory beyond what he had taken from Maxentius in Histria. As the official successor of Severus, Licinius had been tasked with the recovery of Italy, and could so justify an opportunistic strike against the territory captured by Constantine. And what if Constantine failed to reduce Rome by siege and was forced to retreat? In AD 307, Constantine had declined Maximian's invitation to attack Galerius as he retreated from Rome, but Licinius, despite his betrothal to Constantia and alliance with Constantine, was unlikely to have allowed scruples to interfere with the opportunity to eliminate a rival if a similar situation presented itself in late AD 312 or early 313 (see Lact. *DMP* 50–51 for Licinius' ruthlessness).

Early 20th-century view of the Milvian Bridge with the Monte Mario in the background. (RHC Archive)

Fortunately for Constantine, Maxentius did not stand siege but instead rushed out to his destruction on the sixth anniversary of his usurpation, i.e. 28 October AD 312. According to the anonymous orator at Treveri, Maxentius was driven to this rash (but for Constantine, entirely welcome) decision by 'the divine spirit and the eternal majesty of the City [of Rome]' (*Pan. Lat.* 12(9).16.2, 6; *CIL* I² p. 274 for the date). That the divine spirit is unnamed reflects the pagan orator's uncertainty concerning Constantine's adoption of Christianity. Despite the supplies he had collected, it is worth noting that Maxentius' attention to the state of Rome's defences may have lapsed after AD 307. He certainly repaired Aurelian's Wall (Lact. *DMP* 27.1), but the Chronographer of 354 records that another defensive measure, a ditch or moat, was never completed (*Chr. Min.* I 148).

Maxentius' rashness extended to his deployment of his army: 'no one could escape … no one driven from his position could withdraw and fight anew … since he would be restrained in front by weapons and in the rear by the River Tiber' (*Pan. Lat.* 12(9)16.3). The battlefield selected by Maxentius was evidently in close proximity to the Pons Mulvius – the Milvian Bridge (*ibid*. 12(9).17.1).

In the days running up to the battle, the orator tells us, Maxentius had become fatalistic and determined on death for himself and his henchmen. On 26 October, he moved out of the palace on the Palatine Hill and established himself, Valeria, and their surviving son (his name is not recorded) in a private house elsewhere in the city (*Pan. Lat.* 12(9).6.4–5). It was presumably at this time that Maxentius' imperial regalia (standards, spears and sceptres) were boxed up and concealed underground on the Palatine. In this endeavour Maxentius was completely successful; the regalia lay undiscovered for 1,700 years (Panella 2011).

The battle between Maxentius and Constantine was evidently brief. The orator describes how Maxentius' men faltered at the first charge of Constantine's army and immediately fled in panic for the Milvian Bridge, but their escape was hampered by the narrowness of the bridge. Rather than be massacred on the bank by Constantine's soldiers, many of the fugitives

Rome and environs

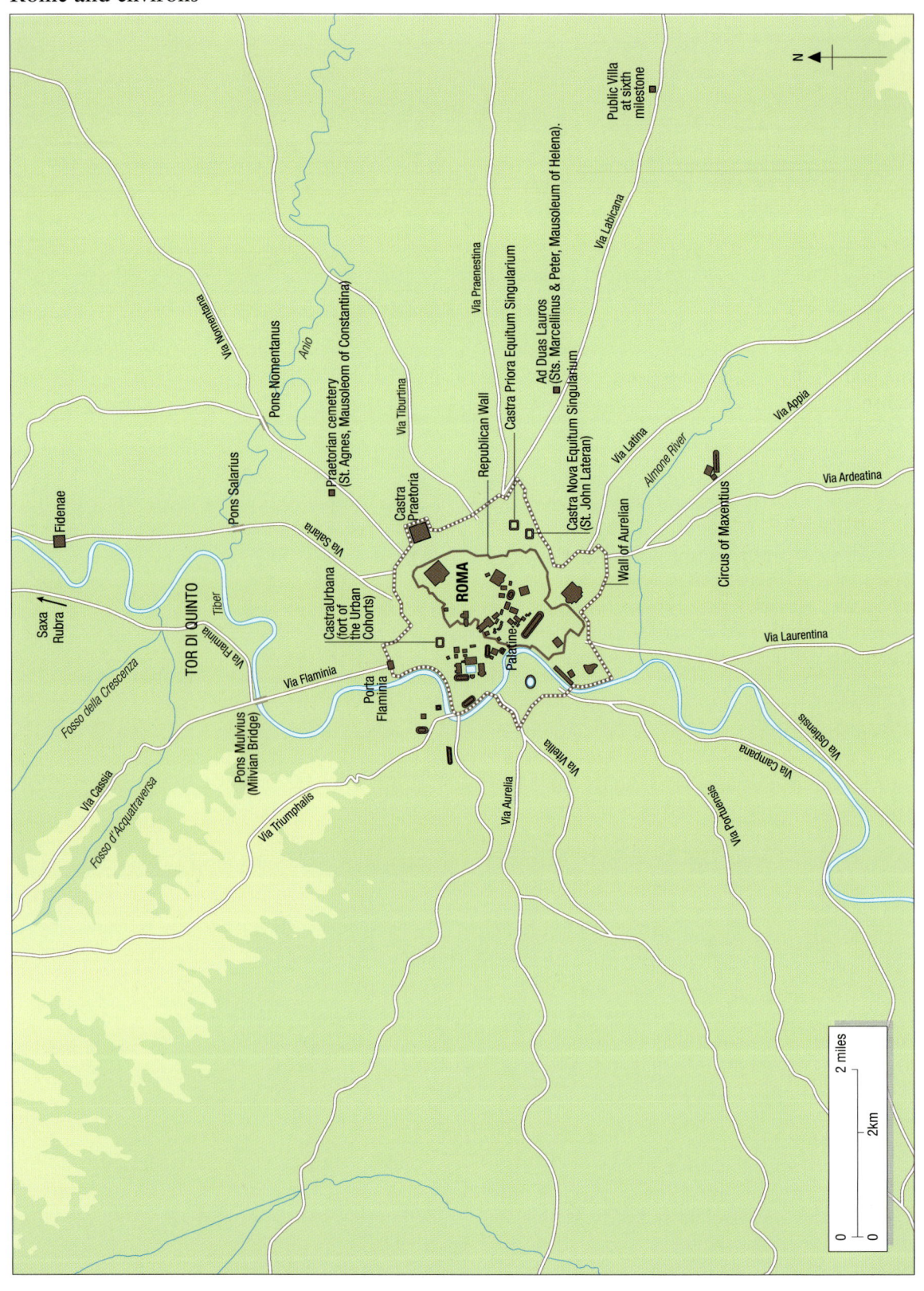

preferred to take their chances crossing the fast-flowing Tiber. The only Maxentians to stand their ground and put up a fight were 'the first instigators of that usurpation who in despair of pardon covered with their bodies the place they had chosen for combat' (*Pan. Lat.* 12(9).17.1). These first instigators must be identified as the Praetorian Guard, who had been the principal supporters of Maxentius' elevation exactly six years before. Their last stand was very much in the tradition of the Guard, recalling the defiance of Vitellius' praetorians in AD 69 (Tac. *Hist.* 3.84).

The orator says nothing of Maxentius' role in the battle, except that rather than face an honourable death in combat with a Constantinian soldier, he attempted to escape by fording the river Tiber on his horse. In December AD 69, Flavian cavalry successfully forded the Tiber near the Milvian Bridge, despite the river being swollen by rain, and then fell on the rear of a Vitellian force stationed on the bridge (Dio 64.19.2; Tac. *Hist.* 3.69 for the rain). But Maxentius' attempt to reach the opposite bank failed and he drowned. While the bodies of other fugitives were carried downstream, Maxentius' corpse, conspicuous in its distinctive armour, was 'held [by the river] in the same place where it had killed him'. The people of Rome were thus left in no doubt that he had not escaped and was dead (*Pan. Lat.* 12(9) 17.2–3).

The Milvian Bridge in the 19th century. Only the four central arches belong to the Roman bridge. (RHC Archive)

2. Lactantius

Lactantius' account of the battle of the Milvian Bridge, in chapter 44 of *On the Deaths of the Persecutors*, was written at Nicomedia in AD 314–15. Between AD 309–10 and 312, Lactantius, a Christian and a professor of Latin rhetoric, was in Gaul as tutor to Crispus, the eldest son of Constantine (Barnes 2011, 176–178). While not an eyewitness, Lactantius' connection with Constantine's court, and the sources he could consequently call upon, renders his account of the battle extremely valuable.

Lactantius says nothing specific about the early stages of the war, except that Maxentius remained in Rome 'on the strength of an oracular reply that he would perish if he went outside its gates, his campaign was being conducted for him by capable *duces* (generals)' (Lact. *DMP* 44.1). He goes on to state that Maxentius' forces outnumbered Constantine's, specifying the army of Maximian, which had deserted from Severus, and Maxentius' own army, which he had recently levied from the Mauri and Italians (Lact. *DMP* 44.2 with Adams & Brennan 1990). This presumably refers to Maxentius' forces at the start of the war; by the time the battle of the Milvian Bridge was fought, the manpower Maxentius could muster was greatly diminished.

Lactantius continues with the intriguing statement that 'Maxentius' troops held the advantage until Constantine at a later stage, his courage renewed and ready either for success or death, moved all his forces nearer the city (of Rome) and based himself in the *regio* (region) of the Milvian Bridge' (Lact. *DMP* 44.3). Despite the close call at Verona, it was Constantine who emerged victorious from every encounter in northern Italy. No other source suggests any success by Maxentius' troops or hints at why Constantine would need to renew his courage but if Lactantius' statement is to be accepted, the advantage held by the Maxentians should refer to a success (or successes) over Constantine's army as it advanced down the Via Flaminia. The memorials to the *Divitenses* at Spoletium and Ocriculum might point to the determined defence of those towns by Maxentian garrisons or even to skirmishes in the Umbrian countryside in which Constantine's vanguard came off worst (Kuhoff 2011, 16–17), but Constantine's renewal of courage and decision to advance to a position just a few kilometres from the gates of Rome alludes, I think, to a Maxentian success much nearer to the capital, perhaps at Saxa Rubra (see **no. 7**, below).

Constantine reached the *regio* of the Milvian Bridge on 27 October. That night he was instructed 'in a dream to mark the heavenly sign of God on the shields of his soldiers and then engage in battle' (Lact. *DMP* 44.4–5). The sign was the Christogram, a combination of the Greek letters X (*chi*) and P (*rho*). The exact form of Christogram, or *Chi-Rho* symbol, employed at the battle of the Milvian Bridge can be seen on a medallion Constantine had minted at Ticinum to celebrate his *decennalia* in AD 315 (see below, **no. 5**).

It should not be doubted that Constantine had such a dream and acted upon it (probably encouraged by Ossius of Corduba). Dreams and visions were powerful motivators in the Roman world, especially for military men. While commanding a vexillation drawn from the legions and auxiliary units of Britannia and the German provinces, the *protector* Vitalianus made a dedication to Jupiter Monitor (Jupiter the Reminder) after having been warned by the god about something in his sleep (*ILS* 546, AD 260–68). In the same period, Aurelius Faustus, also a *protector*, erected an *aedicula* (shrine or small temple) when he experienced a vision of the goddess Valentia at Ocriculum (*ILS* 4002). It is possible that Constantine heard about these very dreams from his father, who had begun his career in the *protectores* around AD 270. The soldier-historian Ammianus Marcellinus, another *protector*, was deeply interested in dreams and portents. He noted how the emperors Constantius II and Julian, the son and nephew of Constantine, experienced dream-visions of *genii*, spirits. Constantius II knew death was near when his guardian spirit stopped appearing to him (Amm. Marc. 21.14.2). Julian's brief reign was framed by dreams of the *Genius Publicus* – the protective spirit of the Roman People. In February AD 360, the spirit spoke supportively to Julian in a dream the night before he was proclaimed emperor. In June AD 363, when his army was encamped for night during the retreat from Persia, Julian dreamt that a mournful Genius Publicus passed through his tent, taking with it the horn of plenty (*ibid*. 20.5.10; 25.2.3–4). The emperor was mortally wounded in a skirmish the next day (*ibid*. 25.3).

The vast majority of Constantine's soldiers were pagan and they prayed to the gods for his safety (*Cod. Theod*. 7.20.2). They understood the great import of a dream sent by a god, but they would also have recalled, indeed some would have participated in, the Great Persecution of the Christians (although Constantius I had limited his actions to demolishing churches) and recognized the *Chi-Rho* as the symbol of a cult that until AD 311 was considered dangerous and un-Roman. And yet on the morning of 28 October Constantine's soldiers formed their line of battle with the mark of Christ hastily daubed over their regular shield blazons. Despite the knowledge that the senior emperor Galerius had issued an edict from his deathbed ending the persecution of the Christians, the soldiers probably remained suspicious of the symbol until it secured the victory Constantine promised.

Maxentius' soldiers then crossed the Tiber to do battle but, according to Lactantius, the emperor was not with them. Evidently allowed to cross the river unopposed, the Maxentians formed their battle line and the two sides then embarked on a formal pitched battle in which neither gave ground (Lact. *DMP* 44.6). Maxentius had remained in the city, holding games, presumably at the Circus Maximus, to celebrate his accession day, but the spectators, emboldened by the appearance of Constantine so near to the Flaminian Gate, chanted 'Constantine cannot be conquered!' Maxentius immediately left the games and called on certain senators and then consulted the sacred Sibylline Books. An oracle worthy of Delphi or Dodona was discovered therein; an enemy of the Romans would perish that day. For all his piety to the old Roman gods, Maxentius was doubtless aware of the ambiguity, but Lactantius asserts the emperor took it as a sign that Constantine, the attacker of Rome, would be defeated. Maxentius then hurried to join his army. He crossed the Milvian Bridge, which was cut down behind him (*ibid*. 44.7–9).

How exactly the demolition of such a major stone structure was achieved is not revealed but that Maxentius should sever his line of retreat in such dramatic fashion was not without precedent. In AD 296, after landing his army on the shore of Britain, the praetorian prefect Asclepiodotus burned his fleet and so signalled there would be no retreat; the army would reconquer the rebellious province or perish in the attempt (*Pan. Lat.* 8(5).15.2). When Julian embarked on the invasion of Persia in AD 363, his army used a bridge of boats to cross the Abora. It was then destroyed, 'so that no soldier ... might entertain hope of a return' (Amm. Marc. 23.5.4–5).

Lactantius has the cutting of the Milvian Bridge done within sight of Maxentius' army; like the anonymous orator of AD 313, he believed the battle was fought close by the bridge. Maxentius' soldiers were momentarily spurred on by the destruction of their avenue of escape, but then 'the Hand of God was over the battle-line.' At this apparent divine intervention, Maxentius' army panicked and turned in flight. The emperor himself fled towards the Milvian Bridge, perhaps hoping that it could still be crossed, but the bridge was broken. Maxentius was swept up by the mass of fugitives and pushed into the Tiber, where he drowned (Lact. *DMP* 44.9).

3. The Arch of Constantine

The Arch of Constantine in Rome was dedicated in the emperor's presence on the occasion of his *decennalia* (assumption of his tenth year of rule) in July AD 315. Although built by the Senate and People of Rome, the inscription and its decoration were likely approved by the emperor. The inscription on the north and south faces of the arch declares how Constantine 'by the inspiration of divinity and the greatness of his own mind, with his army he avenged the state with righteous arms against both the tyrant and all of his

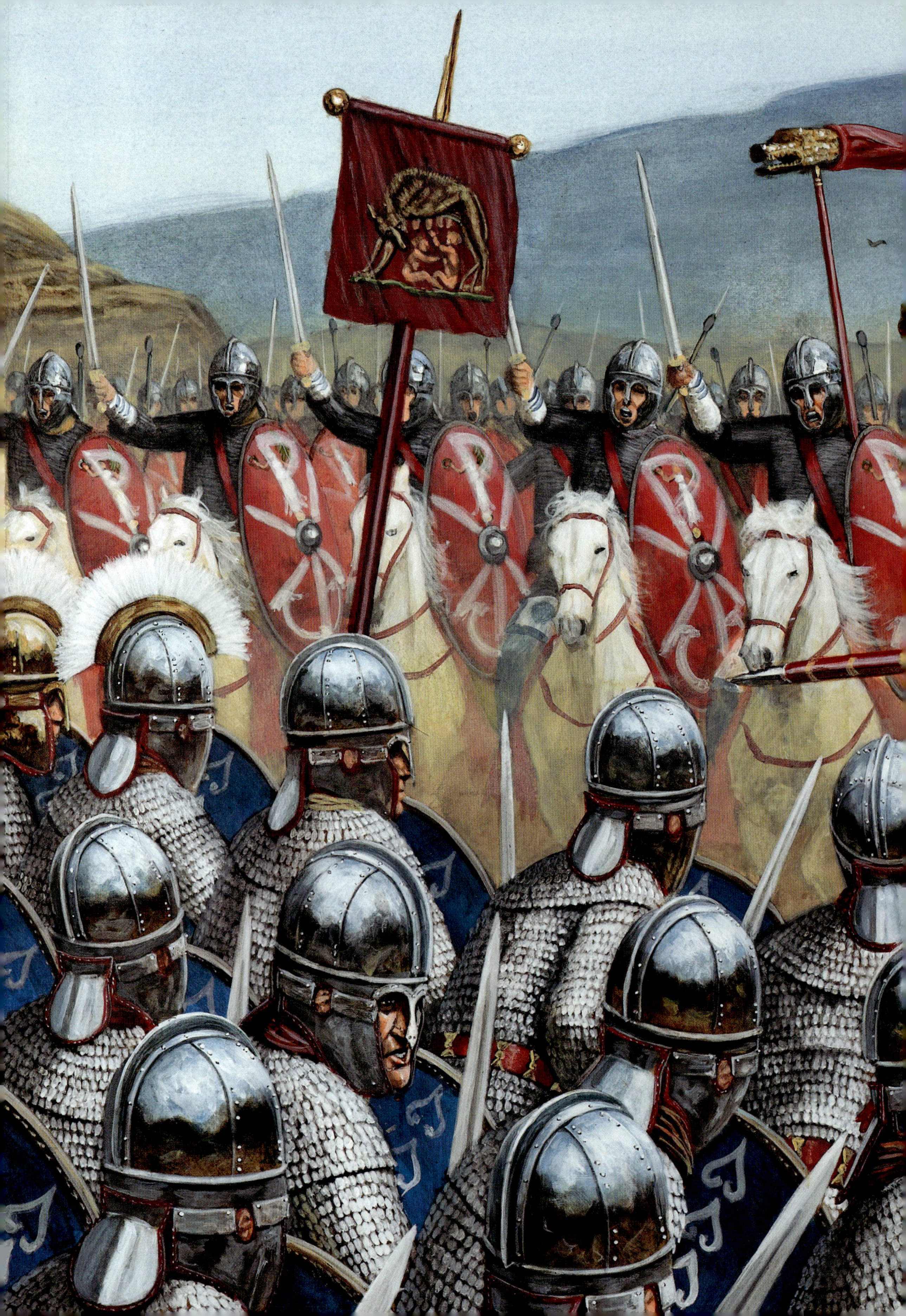

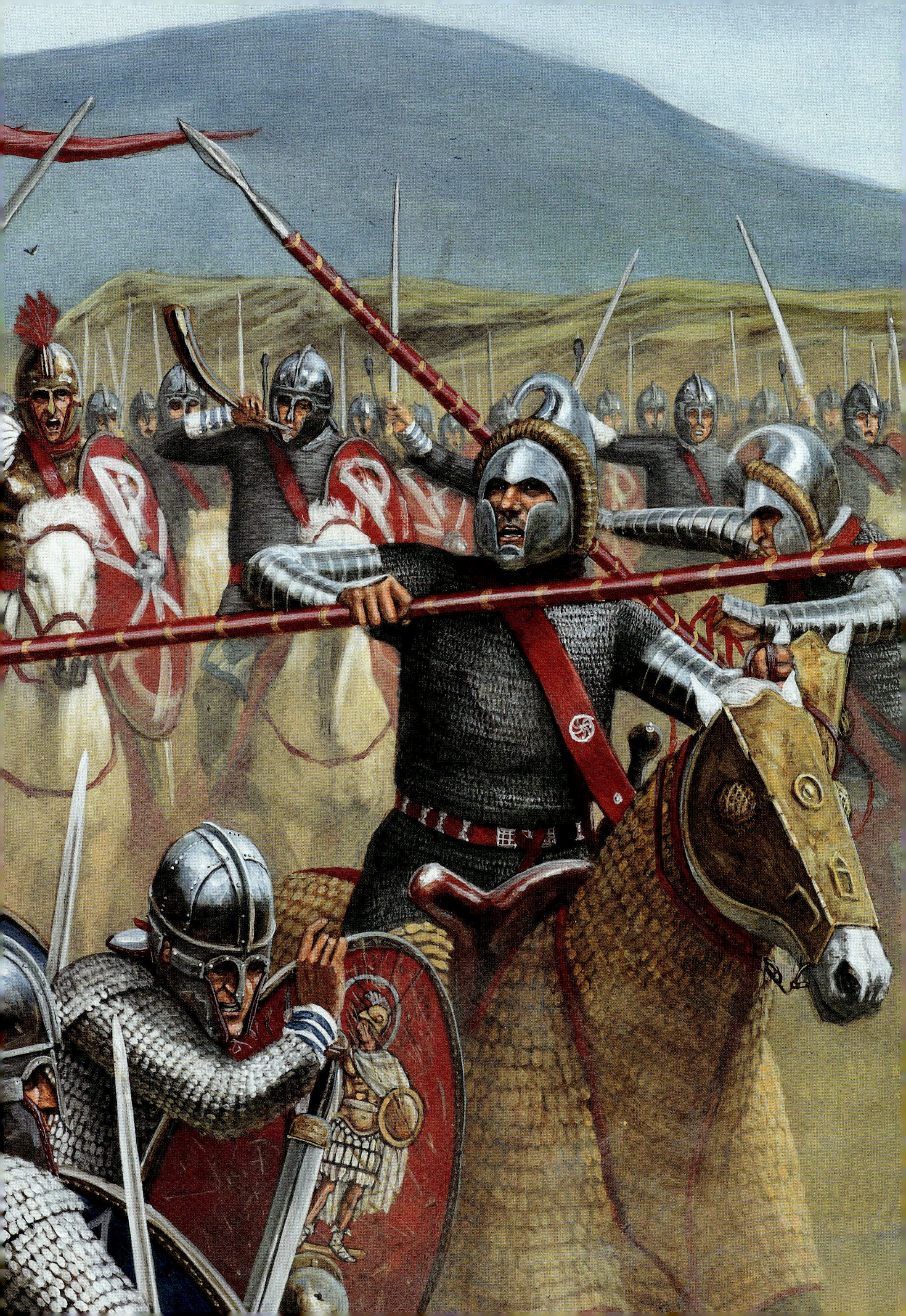

THE BATTLE BEGINS (PP. 50–51)

A cavalry *vexillatio* from the left wing of Constantine's army bears down on Maxentius' leading cavalry division and the top right corner of his infantry *agmen quadratum* (square column).

The Constantinian cavalry are led by a cuirassed tribune (**1**), a *draconarius* (bearer of the unit's dragon standard) (**2**), and a trumpeter who sounds the charge (**3**). The usual shield blazon of the *vexillatio* – Victory and facing animal heads taken from an example on a column base on the Arch of Constantine, has been painted over with the Christogram, the sacred symbol that Constantine has promised will make their victory certain (**4**).

The Maxentian cavalry flee from the *impetus* (charge) of Constantine's divinely inspired warriors. The horsemen are depicted here as fully armoured *clibanarii* ('ovenmen'), like those who fought in the first major battle of the war at Augusta Taurinorum (Turin) (**5**). Their eagle-crested helmets are inspired by the helmet depicted on the gravestone of an *eques singularis* (horse guardsman) who may have been killed in the battle at Brixia (Brescia).

Maxentius' infantry, however, stand firm. They are legionary veterans who served originally with the Augusti Severus and Galerius. They fight under a *vexillum* (banner) decorated with the she-wolf and twins – Romulus and Remus – signifying their role as the true defenders of Rome (**6**).

The Arch of Constantine in Rome, dedicated by the emperor to celebrate his *decennalia* in AD 315. (D. Massaro)

faction at one and the same time' (*ILS* 694). The tyrant is Maxentius. As in the Panegyric of AD 313, the divinity is left unspecified.

The arch is decorated with a mixture of original sculpture and reworked elements from Trajanic, Hadrianic and Antonine monuments, selected from military, hunting and religious scenes that reflected Constantine's martial achievements, his manliness and piety and associated him with the most celebrated of Roman emperors. In the *spolia*, the heads of Trajan, Hadrian and Marcus Aurelius were re-carved with the features of Constantine or his father.

The original decoration of the arch includes column bases of Victories, standard-bearers (some holding *signa* of praetorian type), and soldiers with Germanic captives, reminding viewers of Constantine's defeats of barbarians between AD 306 and 314. Original roundels on the flanks of the arch depict Sol and his divine associate Luna, reflecting Constantine's patron deity prior to his eve-of-battle adoption of Christianity in AD 312. The principal original decoration is the frieze that depicts Constantine's war against Maxentius. The section on the right-hand side of the south face of the arch depicts the battle of the Milvian Bridge.

To the left of the scene, Constantine stands at the edge of one of the broken arches of the Milvian Bridge. The emperor is flanked by Roma, the personified deity of the city of Rome, and Victory, while Father Tiber, the river god, emerges from the water by the emperor's feet. At the far left, an infantryman wearing a helmet decorated with twin horns or feathers at the brow follows the goddess Roma onto the Milvian Bridge.

The battle of the Milvian Bridge Frieze on the Arch of Constantine. (RHC Archive)

MAXENTIUS' ARMY
1. Praetorians and legionaries
2. *Subsidia* (Italian and N. African levies)
3. Regular cavalry (*vexillationes* and *numeri*)
4. Guard cavalry
5. Force of infantry and cavalry guarding road junction at Milvian Bridge

MAXENTIUS

VIA CASSIA

TOR DI QUINTO

VIA TIBERINA/CLODIA

MILVIAN BRIDGE

BRIDGE OF BOATS

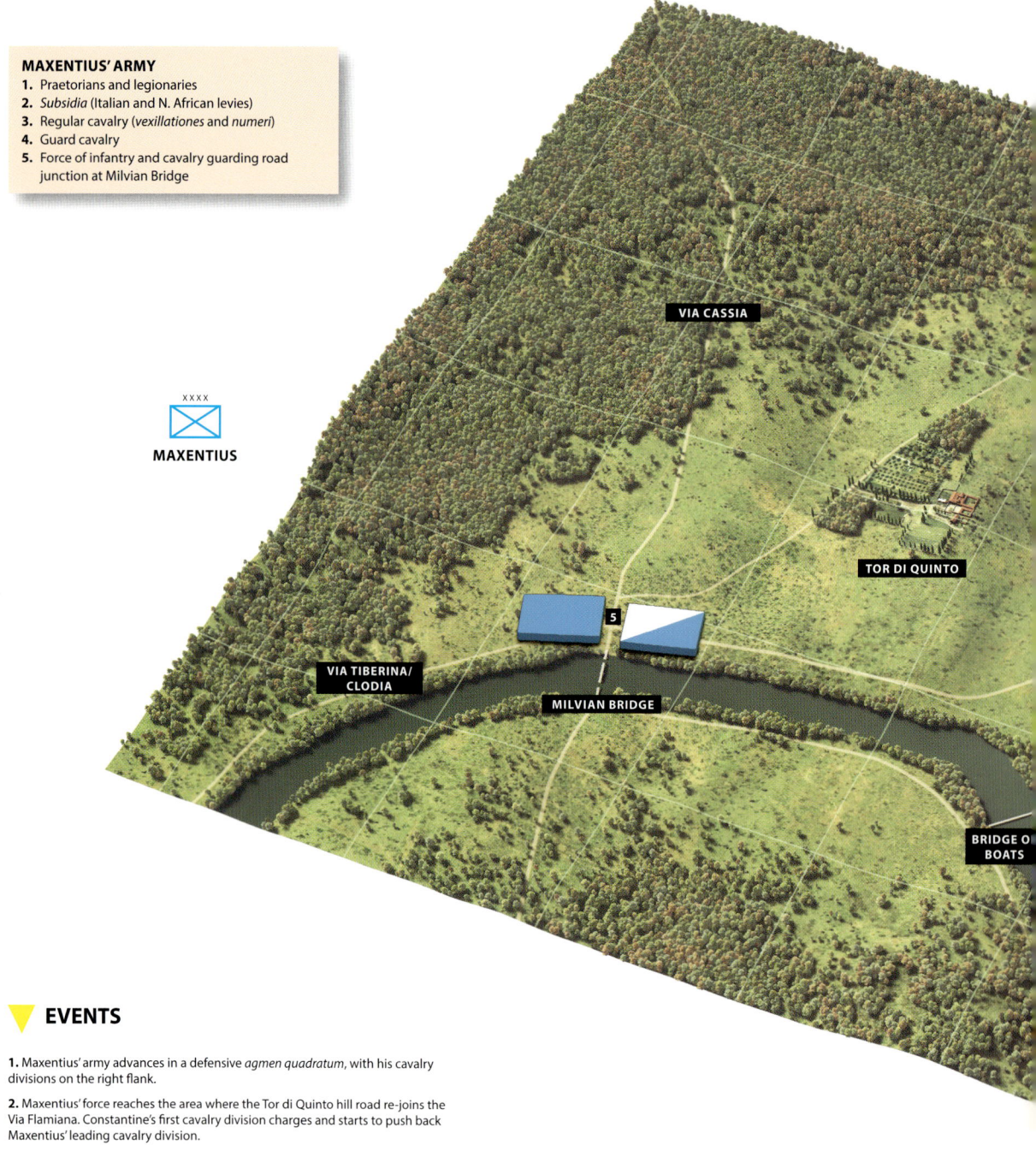

EVENTS

1. Maxentius' army advances in a defensive *agmen quadratum*, with his cavalry divisions on the right flank.

2. Maxentius' force reaches the area where the Tor di Quinto hill road re-joins the Via Flamiana. Constantine's first cavalry division charges and starts to push back Maxentius' leading cavalry division.

3. Constantine's first battle line of infantry charges but is held by Maxentius' veteran praetorians and legionaries.

4. Maxentius' second cavalry division reinforces the first division, slowing the advance of Constantine's cavalry.

OPENING STAGES

Knowing that Maxentius could easily retreat behind the walls of Rome and wait out a siege, Constantine tempts him into open battle by deploying his own army in a disadvantageous position at the north of Tor di Quinto with the river Tiber to its rear. He refrains from attacking Maxentius' bridgeheads on the north bank of the Tiber and makes no attempt to harass Maxentius' army as it uses the bridge of boats to cross over to Tor di Quinto.

Note: Gridlines are shown at intervals of 500m

CONSTANTINE'S ARMY
A. Legionary detachments and *auxilia* (first battle line)
B. Legionary detachments and *auxilia* (second battle line)
C. Cavalry *vexillationes* and *numeri* (left wing, first division)
D. Cavalry *vexillationes* and *numeri* (left wing, second division)
E. Cavalry *vexillations* and *numeri* (right wing)

VIA FLAMINIA

CONSTANTINE

RIVER TIBER

N

Detail of the Milvian Bridge Frieze. The figure of Constantine is almost entirely broken away, but he stands between Roma and Victory on the edge of a broken arch of the Pons Mulvius. (Florian Himmler)

In the centre of the scene, ten Constantinian soldiers (infantry, cavalry and archers) charge (from left to right) along the bank of the Tiber and aim their weapons at ten Maxentian cavalrymen who have been pursued into the river. The Constantinians are clad in tunics and are protected only by helmets and oval shields, but the Maxentian cavalry have short-sleeved shirts of scale body armour. One of the Maxentians is thigh-deep in the water and maintains a defensive posture with his shield and sword, but his fellows are either thrown from their mounts as they are forced into the river, struggle to swim in their armour, or hold out their arms in gestures of supplication towards their pursuers. It has been suggested that the cavalrymen represent Maxentius and his horse guard, but the ten Maxentians are uniformly equipped (Speidel 1986). If the 'tyrant' Maxentius does feature in the scene, he is not distinguished in any obvious manner, such as being armoured like Constantine with a muscle cuirass.

At the right of the scene are two of Constantine's musicians, a *tubicen* (trumpeter) and a *cornicen* (hornist), evidently located upstream of their comrades. They stand on what may be a pontoon and enthusiastically sound the pursuit of the Maxentian fugitives.

Considering the date of the arch and its proximity to the battlefield, whoever conceived the frieze (presumably a group of senators, all of whom would have been in the service of Maxentius until 28 October AD 312) may have been eyewitnesses to the fight, or would certainly have been able to consult participants or observers for details. The frieze confirms the accounts of the anonymous orator of AD 313 and of Lactantius that the battle was fought near the bridge. It also confirms Lactantius' report that the bridge was cut, and that the Maxentians were forced into the Tiber.

4. Eusebius
Eusebius, bishop of Caesarea (*c.* AD 313–39), wrote two accounts of Constantine's battle against Maxentius. The first account is found in the *Ecclesiastical History* (9.9.3–8). This work did not reach its final form until

AD 324, but the section concerning the battle was composed no later than AD 315 (Barnes 2011, 11–12). The second account, in his posthumously published *Life of Constantine* (1.38), was modelled on the earlier version.

Eusebius informs us that Constantine, aided by God, was victorious against three of the tyrant's armies (presumably referring to the Maxentian forces at Segusio, Turin and Verona) and then advanced very near to Rome itself. The emperor, however, was concerned that the tyrant Maxentius would not come out to fight but, happily, God Himself intervened and 'as if with chains dragged the tyrant far away from the gates'. Maxentius emerged from Rome with his guardsmen and regular soldiers and crossed the river (i.e. the Tiber) using a bridge of boats (Euseb. *HE* 9.9.3–5). Contrary to Lactantius' statement, this would indicate that the Milvian Bridge was cut in advance of the battle.

The bridge of boats was to prove Maxentius' undoing. As he crossed, apparently advancing to engage with Constantine, the bridge of boats collapsed and Maxentius and his guardsmen sank like stones (Euseb. *HE* 9.9.5–8). Eusebius implies an act of God and compares Maxentius' fate with that of Pharaoh who perished in the Red Sea when pursuing Moses. In the revised account of the battle in the *Life of Constantine*, the bridge of boats has become a trap that Maxentius intended to use against Constantine, but God triggers the concealed mechanism that causes the construction to break apart while Maxentius is crossing it (Euseb. *VC* 1.38.2–4).

Bishop Eusebius' first account of the battle is contemporary with that of Lactantius, but he does not mention Constantine's dream on the eve of combat and his conversion to or adoption of Christianity. Eusebius assumes that Constantine was already a Christian before he embarked on the invasion of Italy (*HE* 9.9.2). In his second account of the war, Eusebius introduces Constantine's vision of the Cross and related dream and the creation of the *labarum*, the Christian battle standard that added the Christogram and *imagines* of the emperor and his sons to a bejewelled *vexillum*. All this was related to him by Constantine around AD 336 (*VC* 1.28–32). But Constantine's account is highly problematical. The emperor was vague about exactly where and when this vision occurred, only that it happened during a 'campaign somewhere' before the invasion of Italy and was shared by his whole army. It conflates the AD 310 vision of Apollo/Sol (*Pan. Lat.* 6(7).21, now reinterpreted as Christ) with the dream before the battle of the Milvian Bridge. Finally, the *labarum* first appears on Constantine's coinage in AD 326 and was likely introduced as a battle standard during the final war against Licinius in AD 324 (Odahl 1975).

Roman soldiers crossing a bridge of boats on the Column of Marcus Aurelius. Maxentius constructed such a bridge in AD 312. (RHC Archive)

The *Labarum* on a late Constantinian coin. The banner was not used at the Milvian Bridge; Constantine probably devised it in AD 324. (RHC Archive)

5. Nazarius

Latin Panegyric 4(10) was delivered by the famous rhetorician Nazarius in Rome in AD 321. The occasion was the celebration of the *quinquennalia* (assumption of fifth year of imperial power) of the Caesar Crispus. Neither the prince nor Constantine was present, but Nazarius chose to concentrate on Constantine's Italian campaign of AD 312. *Latin* Panegyric 4(10) is actually the second of two speeches about the war that Nazarius made on successive days. The first speech contained a long account of how Constantine defeated Maxentius on the banks of the River Tiber, as Nazarius reminds his audience at 4(10).30.2. This lost speech may well have been the most detailed account of the battle of the Milvian Bridge, but the second, surviving speech contains many points of interest.

Like the orator of AD 313, Nazarius has Maxentius drawn out of Rome by the force of an unspecified divinity, but then he goes on to congratulate Constantine for calling Maxentius out to battle (*Pan. Lat.* 4(10).27.5–6).

Nazarius has Maxentius advance out to battle but his mind is unhinged by fear and this results in an appalling choice of position; Maxentius arrays his troops with the Tiber immediately behind them, the water actually lapping the feet of those in the rearmost ranks. This tactical folly greatly encourages Constantine, who had feared that the battle might not be decisive if Maxentius had an avenue of escape (*Pan. Lat.* 4(10).28.1–4).

Maxentius' army is then described as being so large that its formation was as deep as it was wide (*Pan. Lat.* 4(10).28–4–5). Ancient armies necessarily had to sacrifice depth in order to extend line; Nazarius thus creates a picture of a huge but unwieldy army in a most unfavourable position. However, a formation of equal breadth and depth suggests an *agmen quadratum*, most familiar as the four-sided column employed by armies advancing into hostile territory but also employed in battle (Hdn. 8.1.2–3; Amm. Marc. 29.5.39). Nazarius uses the words *subsidia* (reserves) and *ordines* (ranks) to emphasize the multitude mustered by Maxentius, but it is unlikely Maxentius had any great numerical superiority in the final encounter. In an army organized in the usual two or three *acies* (battle lines), the soldiers in the rearmost line acted as *subsidia*.

Nazarius goes on to praise Constantine's 'marvellous and excellent plan for arraying your soldiers', but unfortunately offers no specific details. There is perhaps a hint in this section that Constantine planned to use some sort of stratagem to conquer Maxentius, but it proved unnecessary because the enemy faltered at the first charge and the battle was won in a very short space of time (*Pan. Lat.* 4(10).29.1, 30.2).

Assisted by 'heavenly armies', an allusion to the divine inspiration that Constantine claimed to have secured his victory, Nazarius has Constantine lead the opening charge. Conspicuous in a gem-encrusted helmet and bearing a golden shield, the emperor spurs ahead of his men. Missiles glance from his shield; he spears the enemy; Maxentians are trampled beneath the hooves of his warhorse. Constantine is glorified as a heroic exemplar of

Obverse of the medallion minted at Ticinum for Constantine's *decennalia* in AD 315. The emperor's jewelled helmet bears the Christogram, the holy sign that he bade his soldiers paint on their shields before the battle of the Milvian Bridge. (N. Kästner, Staatliche Münzsammlung München)

Part of the Great Trajanic Frieze re-used on the Arch of Constantine. Trajan's features were re-cut to resemble Constantine. It is ironic that the reworked scene depicts Constantine surrounded by the Praetorian Guard, the unit he disbanded after the Milvian Bridge. (Florian Himmler)

traditional Roman *labor* (toil), *vis* (power, force) and, above all, *virtus* (excellence and valour). His deeds inspire the soldiers and they strive to emulate him. The slaughter of the Maxentians is such that heaps of bodies line the bank of the Tiber, and the river itself is clogged with corpses and its current is slowed. Maxentius does not die a manly death in combat but flees like a coward and drowns in the Tiber (*Pan. Lat.* 4(10).29–30).

In AD 315, the year in which Constantine began his tenth year of rule and thus celebrated his *decennalia*, he ordered the mint at Ticinum (Pavia) in north Italy to produce a commemorative medallion for distribution to eminent subjects (*RIC* VII Ticinum 36). The obverse of the oversized silver coin depicts the emperor wearing a helmet decorated with gems, like that described by Nazarius, but it is also surmounted with a crest of roundels and the foremost bears the Christogram – Lactantius' 'heavenly sign of God' (Lact. *DMP* 44.5). With his right hand, the emperor holds the reins of his horse. His left grasps a shield bearing the motif of the she-wolf suckling Romulus and Remus, the founders of Rome. A cross-shaped sceptre surmounted by a globe emerges from behind the shield; it is a combination of the Christian cross with the traditional Roman orb symbolizing world domination. Constantine is shown on the reverse addressing his troops from a tribunal. The emperor is cuirassed and holds a trophy of captured arms. The goddess Victory is by his side and military banners (*vexilla*) flutter behind him. The soldiers clustered around the tribunal are cavalry. The dismounted troopers stand beside

The reverse of the Ticinum medallion shows Constantine addressing the cavalrymen who were crucial in his victory over Maxentius. (N. Kästner, Staatliche Münzsammlung München)

59

their horses, and are equipped with crested helmets, round shields and barbed spears. The Christian imagery on the obverse of the coin, combined with traditional Roman motifs, refers to the battle of the Milvian Bridge and Constantine's liberation of Rome from the tyrant Maxentius. The soldiers commemorated on the reverse are those who played the pivotal role in the battle; they are the cavalrymen who followed Constantine in the mad charge described by Nazarius.

The contemporary narrative frieze on the Arch of Constantine depicts the emperor as commander-in-chief, directing his troops from the broken Milvian Bridge. In the central opening of the arch, a re-used panel of the Great Trajanic Frieze shows the emperor Trajan (r. AD 98–117) charging down Dacian warriors. He is accompanied by another horseman and praetorian infantry come up behind. Trajan's features were re-cut to resemble Constantine and an inscription above the panel reads 'Liberator of the City (of Rome)' (*ILS* 694, 2). The panel was intended to remind viewers of Constantine's personal role in the fighting at the battle of Milvian Bridge where, as Nazarius relates, he led from the front and rode down the enemy.

6. *The Origin of Constantine*

The Origin of Constantine is a brief but well-informed account of Constantine's life. It was composed shortly after the emperor's death in AD 337 (Barnes 2011, 27). The anonymous author tells us that, having defeated the tyrant's generals at Verona, Constantine advanced on Rome. Maxentius then left the city and chose the battleground where he would fight Constantine: a *campus* (field, plain) above the Tiber. Maxentius was defeated at this place and fled, but, being caught up in the mass of fugitives, he was thrown from his horse into the Tiber and drowned (*Origo* 4.12).

There is no mention in the account of the Milvian Bridge, but if we are to look for a *campus* in the vicinity of the bridge and on the right bank of the river, the most likely contenders are Farnesina district, immediately to the east of the bridge at the foot of the Monti della Farnesina, and the more extensive Tor di Quinto, traversed by the Via Flaminia in the bend of the river to the east and north-east.

Early 19th-century view of Prima Porta (Saxa Rubra), showing the buttresses of the Villa of Livia above the floodplain of the Tiber. (RHC Archive)

7. Aurelius Victor

Aurelius Victor was a senior bureaucrat in the imperial civil service. His short history, *The Caesars*, covering the period from Augustus to Constantius II, was published in AD 361.

Victor's brief notice of the battle informs us that Maxentius advanced from Rome to meet Constantine. At Saxa Rubra, at the ninth milestone from Rome (the distance was measured from the old Servian Wall), Maxentius' battle line was cut and he fled back to Rome. But when crossing the Tiber, he was caught in the ambush he had prepared for Constantine at the Milvian Bridge (Aur. Vict. 40.23).

Despite its brevity, Victor's account of the battle has had considerable influence to the extent that many refer not to the battle of the Milvian Bridge, but to the battle of Saxa Rubra.

In Victor's notice, Maxentius falls into his own trap at the Milvian Bridge. That Maxentius had some devious plan to destroy Constantine's army as it crossed the Tiber appears in Eusebius' revised account of the battle, where Maxentius' bridge of boats is rendered into a giant booby-trap (VC 1.38). This presumably reflected Constantine's later propaganda, for the image of the rigged bridge is implied in Photius' summary of Praxagoras' lost *History of Constantine* (*FGrH* 219; Praxagoras was writing *c*. AD 330). In a speech delivered in honour of Constantius II in AD 344, the orator Libanius declares that Maxentius did not dare face the emperor's father in battle 'but pursued his struggle with guile, by his technique in bridging the river, when the contrivance did no harm to those against whom it was devised, but sufficed for the destruction of its creator and, as the proverb goes, he was surrounded and caught in his own schemes' (Lib. *Or.* 59.20). Victor's ambush thus follows a tradition established later in the reign of Constantine, but is conspicuously absent from the earliest accounts of the battle and the idea of a deliberate trap can be dismissed.

Victor's account of the battle suggests a plausible scenario of a main engagement at Saxa Rubra and a pursuit of the defeated Maxentians down the Via Flaminia to the Milvian Bridge. According to Ashby, when Victor's account is combined with Zosimus' description of the battlefield (a broad plain suitable for cavalry: Zos. 2.16.1; see below, **no. 9**) and the emphasis of the *Latin Panegyrics* that the Maxentians had the Tiber at their rear, the floodplain lying between the Via Flaminia and the river immediately east and north of Saxa Rubra (modern Prima Porta) is 'the only position … Maxentius could have taken up which satisfies the conditions laid down by our accounts' (Ashby & Fell 1921, 149–150 following Toebelmann 1915).

Antonio Nibby was the first archaeologist to identify this area as the site of Victor's battlefield (1837, 34–35, 39), but Field Marshal von Moltke preferred the high ground to the west of

The Arch of Malborghetto was converted into a fortress in the middle ages and subsequently used as a farmhouse. The arch certainly dates to the era of Diocletian and Constantine but suggestions that it marks the site of Constantine's *praetorium* before the battle of the Milvian Bridge are fanciful. (MM)

Saxa Rubra (now occupied by Labaro and Prima Porta) as the area where Maxentius formed his army while Constantine waited on the floodplain below (Moltke 1879, 115–122). This was certainly a more secure position for the Maxentians, but it would put the river Cremera (mod. Valchetta) to their rear and the Tiber on their right flank and this contradicts the *Panegyrics* which emphasize that the Tiber was behind them.

Subsequent investigators preferred to return the action to the floodplain. Felice Grossi-Gondi had Maxentius occupy the Villa of Livia (on a hill overlooking Saxa Rubra at the junction of the Via Flaminia and Via Tiberina) and array his army eastwards into the plain. Fritz Toebelmann pushed Maxentius' army a little distance up the Via Flaminia, anchoring the left wing of the army on the road and extending the battle line north-eastwards across what is now the Cimitero Flaminio and on to the bank of the Tiber (Grossi-Gondi 1912; Toebelmann 1915, 22–30). In both cases, the great meanders of the Tiber would carry the river round the rear of Maxentius' army and so comply with the description in the *Panegyrics*. Despite Lactantius placing Constantine's final camp in the region of the Milvian Bridge, Toebelmann also identified the early-4th-century arch at Malborghetto, just past the 13th milestone of the Via Flaminia, as marking the very site of Constantine's *praetorium* (camp headquarters) on the eve of the battle, the place where he had been inspired by God (*ibid*. 30–31). However, the exact date and purpose of the arch remains uncertain. No inscription survives. Arthur Frothingham, who prised from the arch a brick with a stamp on it that indicated manufacture during the reign of Diocletian, rejected any connection with the battle of AD 312 as 'absurd'. He believed the arch marked 'the boundary of the jurisdiction of the urban magistrates in Diocletian's reorganization of Italy' (1915, 159). Whatever its purpose, Constantine passed this way when he accompanied Diocletian to Rome in AD 303 (Barnes 1981, 25). When he advanced on the capital nine years later, the terrain of the Tiber Valley was not unfamiliar to him.

Kromayer and Veith's plan of the battle of the Allia (390 BC), fought in the Tiber Valley opposite Saxa Rubra. Despite the report of Aurelius Victor, the battle of the Milvian Bridge was not fought here. (RHC Archive)

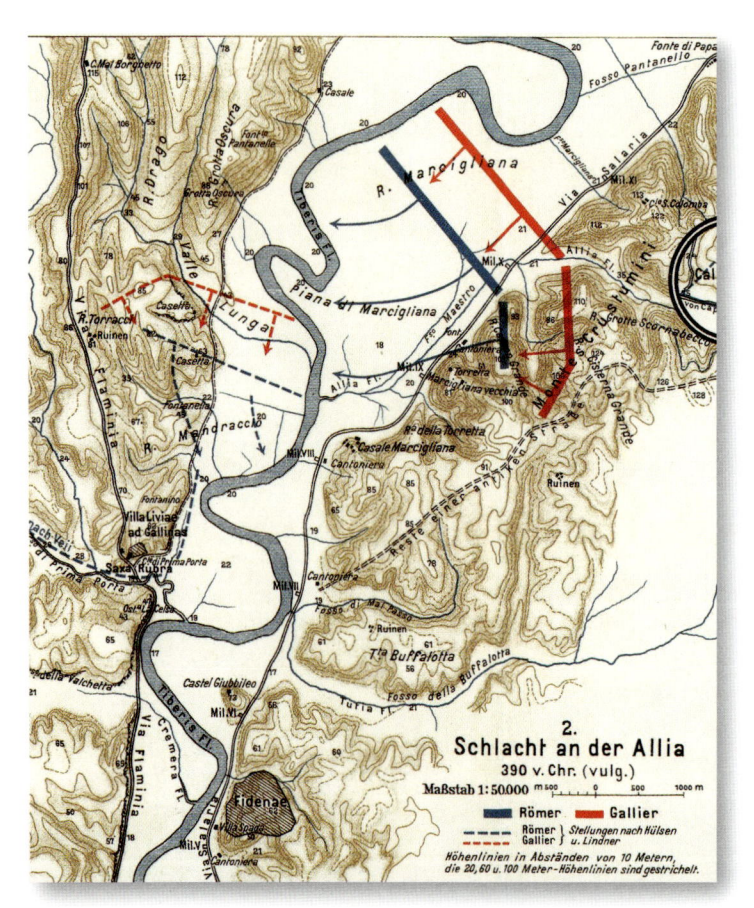

Otto Seeck did not accept that the decisive battle was fought at Saxa Rubra with a secondary encounter involving the fugitives at the Milvian Bridge. Victor's account suggested to Seeck that Maxentius' army was attacked while still in column as it marched up the Via Flaminia; the head of the column being pinned down at Saxa Rubra while its rear was attacked by forces that Constantine had sent down the Via Cassia – easily accessed by routes leading to Veii – to the

Milvian Bridge (Seeck 1921, 131–134; cf. Costa 1913, 206 for a secondary Constantinian force being sent up the Cremera Valley to access the Via Cassia and then fall on the Pons Mulvius). This scenario is also plausible. Severan generals won the battle of Issus (AD 194), and perhaps Lugdunum (AD 197), by sending large cavalry forces on long detours to outflank the enemy and attack them in the rear (Dio 74.7.4; 75.6.8). Grossi-Gondi placed the main battle on the plain by Saxa Rubra but, following the battle scene on the Arch of Constantine, he believed that Constantine had sent a detached force to reach the Milvian Bridge and so cut off the retreat of Maxentian fugitives to Rome or Trans Tiberim (Trastevere) (1912, 401–403).

More recently, Kuhoff has suggested that Maxentius' army marched to Saxa Rubra but was promptly pushed back to its second position by the bridge of boats near the Pons Mulvius. He believes Maxentius' commanders were not seeking a decisive encounter but wanted to slow Constantine's advance and to inflict casualties before they retreated behind the walls of Rome. However, Maxentius emerged from the city and the defensive action on the north bank of the Tiber at the bridge of boats turned into a rout in which the emperor drowned as he attempted to flee (Kuhoff 1991, 147–162).

Aurelius Victor is the only ancient source to mention Saxa Rubra as the site, or at least the starting point, of the final encounter between Constantine and Maxentius. The absence of Saxa Rubra from the other accounts of the battle is curious, for it was a famous place, not least as the site of the palatial Villa of Livia, the first empress (Pl. *NH* 15.136–137; Vistoli 2010, 113–153).

It has been suggested that Victor (or his source) was simply mistaken about the battle at Saxa Rubra, or confused it with an earlier, unhistorical encounter (Moreau 1952). Victor also reports a battle at the Milvian Bridge between Didius Julianus and Septimius Severus in AD 193 (Aur. Vict. 19.3), but there was no such battle, for Julianus was abandoned by his troops, condemned by the Senate and executed before Severus reached Rome (Dio 73.17; Hdn. 2.12). Septimius did, however, face a mutiny over poor camp conditions at Saxa Rubra, and the Praetorian Guardsmen who had elevated and then disposed of Julianus were surrounded, stripped of military insignia and dishonourably disbanded at Saxa Rubra (HA *Sev.* 8.9; Dio 74.1; Hdn. 2.13).

The name Saxa Rubra (Red Rocks) referred to the colour of the tufa cliffs that rose up immediately south of the settlement and loomed above the Via Flaminia for several kilometres as it followed the floor of the Tiber Valley towards Rome. Armies, like that of Severus, found ample room to camp in the plain immediately to the north, but continuing the advance on Rome meant traversing the bottleneck

Aerial reconnaissance photo of Tor di Quinto in 1943. The Milvian Bridge is in the bottom left corner. This plain, in a loop of the Tiber, was the location of the battle in AD 312. (SDASM Archives)

between the red rock cliffs and the river. Recalling Lactantius' statement concerning a Maxentian success prior to Constantine renewing his courage and advancing to the region of the Milvian Bridge (Lact. *DMP* 44.3), Landmann argued that Saxa Rubra was actually the location of the defeat of Constantine's vanguard as it attempted to force the bottleneck. This would have occurred some days before the battle of the Milvian Bridge and is the source of the confusion that the battle of the Milvian Bridge started at Saxa Rubra (Landmann 1913, 148). Constantine's propaganda may well have recast Saxa Rubra as a victory that became conflated with the final encounter by the Milvian Bridge.

Landmann thought that the camp established by Constantine in the Milvian Bridge region was not on the plain of Tor di Quinto, but on the high ground to the west between the Via Cassia and the Via Flaminia. He believed that Constantine did not sweep down from the hills to attack Maxentius' men while they were crossing the bridge of boats but allowed the whole army to deploy at Farnesina where, with no means of retreat, it could be more easily destroyed (Landmann 1913, 149–150; Moreau 1952, 372).

The field of Farnesina is, however, too constricted to be identified with the plain that Zosimus described as being suitable for cavalry (see **no. 9**, below). Costa argued that the more expansive plain of Tor di Quinto, only a kilometre upstream of the Milvian Bridge and traversed by the Via Flaminia, was the only site that meets the requirements of a battlefield very close to the Pons Mulvius that was suitable for cavalry and would place the Tiber to the rear of Maxentius's army (Costa 1913, 200–204).

8. *Epitome de Caesaribus*

The author of the *Epitome of the Caesars* is not known, but his work appeared in the late AD 360s or 370s. He informs readers that Maxentius was galloping across a bridge of boats, located just a little upstream of the Milvian Bridge, to meet Constantine in battle, when his horse slipped and plunged

The Milvian Bridge region in 2011, illustrating modern development at Farnesina/Foro Italico and on the high ground of Tor di Quinto where the *horti* of Ovid were located. (Doc Searls)

into the Tiber. Maxentius drowned because of his heavy body armour (*thorax*) and it was only with difficulty that his corpse was recovered (*Epit.* 40.7).

That Maxentius was crossing the bridge of boats en route to battle, rather than fleeing from it, suggests that the Pons Mulvius had been cut prior to the battle (*contra* Lactantius, **no. 2**, above). In the *Epitome* the bridge of boats (*pontem navigiis compositum*) is simply a means of transporting Maxentius and his soldiers to the battlefield; it is not a device intended for the destruction of Constantine's men.

Grossi-Gondi thought the bridge of boats was in direct alignment with the Via Flaminia where it enters the plain of Tor di Quinto (1912, 401), while Costa preferred to locate the southern end a little farther upstream at Acqua Acetosa (1913, 206). The present writer suggests it was located about a kilometre upstream of the Pons Mulvius, before the high ground of the Parco di Villa Glori, and connected with the north (or right) bank just below Parco Tor di Quinto.

9. Zosimus

Zosimus, an imperial bureaucrat, composed his *New History* of the Roman Empire in Greek at the turn of the 5th and 6th centuries AD. Zosimus was far removed from the events of AD 312, but he relied on sources now lost to us, including Eunapius (b. *c.* AD 345), a Greek historian who was critical of Constantine.

After detailing the exaggerated sizes of the opposing forces at the start of the war (Constantine with 90,000 infantry and 8,000 cavalry; Maxentius with 170,000 infantry and 18,000 cavalry: Zos. 2.15.1–2), Zosimus describes a wooden bridge that Maxentius constructed as a trap for Constantine:

> Maxentius threw a bridge over the Tiber, which was not of one entire piece, but divided into two parts, the centre of the bridge being made to fasten with iron pins, which might be drawn out upon occasion. He gave orders to the engineers, that as soon as they saw the army of Constantine upon the juncture of the bridge, they should draw out the iron fastenings, that the enemy who stood upon it might fall into the river. (Zosimus 2.15.3–4)

Zosimus then returns to Constantine, informing readers that the emperor had advanced to the outskirts of Rome and established camp in a broad plain that was suitable for the manoeuvres of cavalry (Zos. 2.16.1). Maxentius sheltered behind the walls of Rome and consulted the Sybilline Books. He found 'a prediction that whoever designed any harm to the Romans should die a miserable death'. Considering himself to be the defender of Rome, Maxentius took this omen to refer to Constantine, promptly led his army out of the city and crossed the rigged bridge to the plain where Constantine was encamped (Zos. 2.16.1–2). As Costa argued, this plain is to be identified with Tor di Quinto (cf. Moreau 1952, 372–373).

As Maxentius' army crossed the Tiber, Constantine formed his men into battle order and waited for the enemy to deploy into line. He then opened the action by launching his cavalry against Maxentius' horse, which was thrown into disorder. Constantine signalled his infantry to advance. They charged into the ranks of the Maxentian infantry and fought furiously. The Italian and African conscripts were loath to risk their lives for a hated tyrant and gave way, but Maxentius' other troops (here Zosimus alludes to the praetorians and the veteran legionaries Maxentius acquired from Severus) refused to retreat and were either trampled by Constantine's cavalry or cut down by the infantry (Zos. 2.16.2–3).

Zosimus has Maxentius' cavalry defeated at the start of the battle and his infantry conscripts give up the fight almost immediately; the emperor's regular troops stand their ground but are slaughtered. The battle should be over, but at 2.16.4 Zosimus tells us that 'as long as the cavalry kept their ground, Maxentius retained some hope.' We must assume that Maxentius had a second force of cavalry that came into action, perhaps the emperor's own horse guard. However, this force of cavalry also gave way and Maxentius joined in the flight towards the bridge that he had intended as an engine for the destruction of Constantine's army. Even with the iron pins still in place, the bridge could not withstand the weight of the fugitives and its timbers broke. Maxentius was thrown into the Tiber and swept downstream (Zos. 2.16.4).

TOR DI QUINTO AND THE ARCHAEOLOGY OF THE MILVIAN BRIDGE REGION

The plain of Tor di Quinto, which takes its name from the medieval Torre (tower) di Quinto that stands on a rocky outcrop above the fifth milestone of the Via Flaminia, opens up approximately a kilometre upstream of the Milvian Bridge. The plain extends about 2km north to the confluence of the Fossi d'Acquatraversa and della Crescenza at Due Ponti. The width of the plain from west to east varies from about 1 to 2km. The plain, which sits 16–17m above sea level, is bounded to the north, east and south by the river Tiber. The plain is overlooked by hills to the west, some sheer sided, rising to a maximum of about 50m above sea level. A *diverticulum* (side road) spurs off the Via Flaminia just south of the Torre di Quinto outcrop to cross the high ground and join the Via Cassia at the north end of the Milvian Bridge. This was the *regio* of the Pons Mulvius (Vistoli 2010; Rossi 2012; Messineo 2003).

In AD 69, the army of Vitellius, comprising some 60,000 legionaries and auxiliaries and an even greater number of camp followers, bivouacked at Tor di Quinto (Tac. *Hist*. 2.87–88; Wellesley 2000, 101–102). Later that year, the Flavian general Antonius Primus wished to camp in the same area before crossing the Milvian Bridge and launching his attack on Vitellian Rome (Tac. *Hist*. 3.82). The plain of Tor di Quinto is not vast, but the area is certainly large enough to contain the *c*.40,000–50,000 men who fought at the battle of the Milvian Bridge in AD 312.

The *diverticulum* that crossed the high ground between the Flaminian and Cassian Ways acted as an alternative route when the Tiber burst its banks and the plain of Tor di Quinto was flooded. It also serviced the famous villa and gardens of the poet Ovid. He was exiled to Tomis on the Black Sea in AD 8 and wrote longingly about his estate in the pine-clad hills between the Via Clodia (i.e. the southern end of the Via Cassia) and the Via Flaminia, where he had worked in the *horti* (gardens) and planted orchards and irrigated crops (Ov. *Pont*. 1.43–48). Ovid's villa has not yet been discovered but would have been located on a high point to take in the views of Rome and the Tiber Valley and out of earshot of the noisy main roads and river port at the

The archaeology of the Milvian Bridge and Tor di Quinto

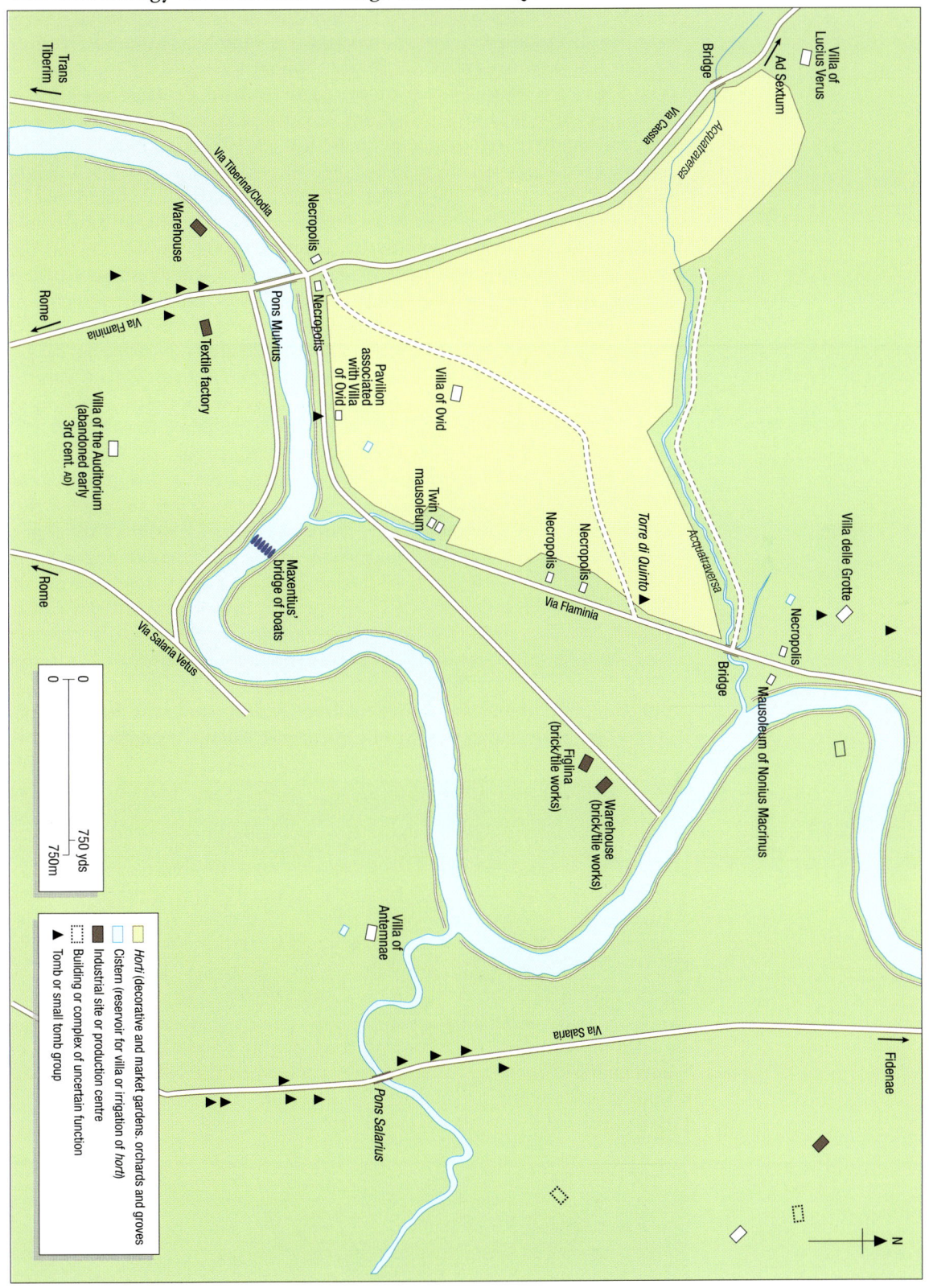

Milvian Bridge (Mart. *Epigr.* 4.64.18–24). A large cistern for the irrigation of crops has been found at Via A. Fleming and, at the foot of the hill, where Viale Tor di Quinto overlies the ancient Via Flaminia, a grand riverside pavilion has been excavated. Both are thought to belong to the estate of Ovid. The *horti* would have comprised decorative gardens and market gardens for the supply of Rome. *Horti* were characterized by high divisional walls and interconnected sunken lanes (Liv. 26.10.6; Tac. *Hist.* 3.82) and snagging brambles (Suet. *Ner.* 48.3).

The produce from Ovid's market gardens could have been taken by cart into Rome by the Via Flaminia. In the 1st and 2nd centuries AD, having descended by the *diverticulum* to the junction of the Via Cassia and Via Flaminia, the carter would have passed through a large cemetery before reaching the north end of the Milvian Bridge. At the end of the 1st century AD, and into the early 2nd, this necropolis was one of the preferred burial grounds of the Praetorian Guard. Caristicus Redemtus, *plumbarius* (water engineer) of the third praetorian cohort, Lucilius Proculus, *fisci curator* (financial clerk) of the sixth cohort, and Ladinius Modestus, *speculator Augusti* (bodyguard of the emperor), were among the praetorians buried here (*AE* 1979, 89; 1984, 68; *CIL* VI 2683). Other notable residents of this necropolis included Parthian and Osrhoenian princes, and a queen of the Costoboci (*ILS* 842, 857, 854).

As the carter progressed over the Milvian Bridge, he would have seen a busy river port below, with stone wharves on both banks and a huge warehouse a little downstream on the left bank. The river would have been packed with vessels taking goods and passengers up-and downstream (Strab. *Geog.* 5.2.5; Tac. *Ann.* 3.9.2). Building materials, for which Rome was always hungry, were carried down the river. Timber was felled in Etruria and floated down to Rome (Strab. *Geog.* 5.2.10). Bricks made from clay dug from the Tiber floodplain were loaded onto barges and sent downstream. There was a *figlina* (brickworks) and warehouse where the hippodrome now

Van Bloemen's early 18th-century view of Tor di Quinto from Acqua Acetosa. (Joanbanjo)

stands on Tor di Quinto. It was connected to the Via Flaminia by a *diverticulum*, and this probably continued to a wharf on the river bank. Close to where this *diverticulum* veered off from the Via Flaminia, the plain was dominated by a monumental double mausoleum. Tombs flanked the Via Flaminia all the way from the Flaminian Gate at Rome to Saxa Rubra, but there was a major concentration at Tor di Quinto. Another great mausoleum may have stood on the spur at the north of the plain and provided a foundation for the medieval Torre di Quinto and, across the twin-arched bridge at the confluence of the Acquatraversa and Crescenza (perhaps demolished by Maxentius to slow Constantine's advance), there was another cemetery and mausoleum complex, including the impressive temple-tomb of Nonius Macrinus, the general of the Marcomannic Wars.

Returning to our carter, after crossing the Milvian Bridge he would have encountered more tombs and buildings. The emperor Nero (AD 54–68) had come here to enjoy 'nocturnal allurements' (Tac. *Ann.* 13.47.2), perhaps in taverns and brothels servicing the river port. Continuing, the carter would have passed an old textile factory and the lane leading to the ancient Villa of the Auditorium and its *horti*. This villa, dating back to the 6th century BC, was probably one of those used by Cicero to conceal his men before apprehending the Allobroges on the Milvian Bridge in 63 BC (Cic. *Cat.* 3.5–6).

By AD 312, the Villa of the Auditorium had been abandoned for about a century or more and the site was used in Late Antiquity for burials. The textile factory had long ceased to operate, as had the brickworks on the plain of Tor di Quinto. But this was still a busy area, with considerable road and river traffic; Maxentius would have had no difficulty in requisitioning vessels and timbers for his bridge of boats. Some of the great villas and estates in the vicinity, such as the Villa of Livia at Saxa Rubra, continued to function, and it is likely that the *horti* on the high ground above the plain of Tor di Quinto continued to produce fruit and vegetables for the huge market of Rome. Although Zosimus describes the plain of Tor di Quinto as broad and suitable for cavalry (Zos. 2.16.1), it was not without obstructions, such as the great double mausoleum and lesser tombs, and whatever remained of the *figlina*.

Reinhart's 1808 view of the Tiber Valley from Acqua Acetosa. The plain of Tor di Quinto and Grottarossa are to the left. (ArishG)

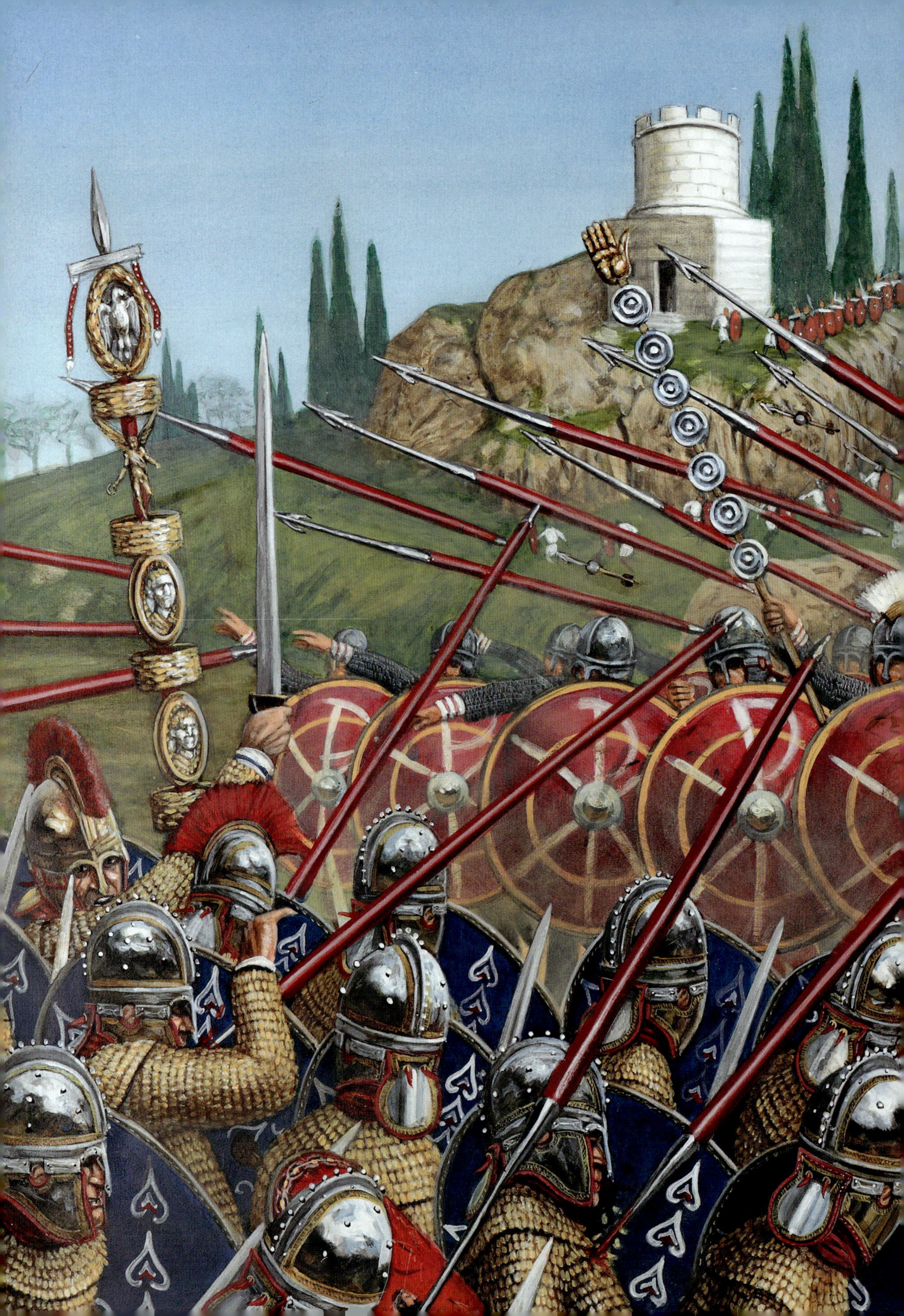

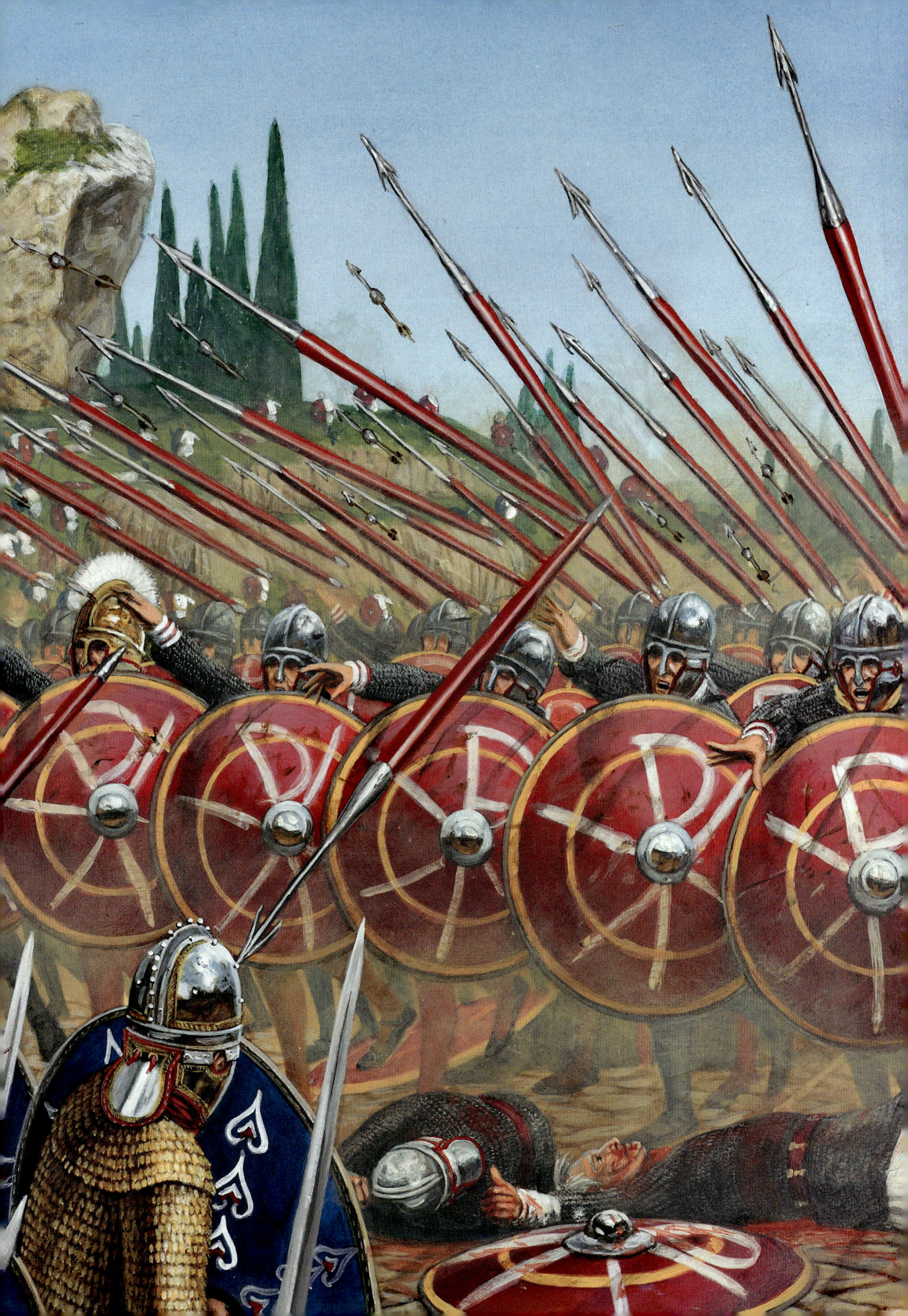

THE INFANTRY BATTLE (PP. 70–71)

Praetorians (**1**), at the top left corner of Maxentius' *agmen quadratum*, and legionaries, on the far right wing of Constantine's army (**2**), clash at the fifth milestone of the Via Flaminia (**3**). Centuries later, a medieval tower would be built on the foundations of the mausoleum on the rocky outcrop overlooking the road – the Torre di Quinto, from which the modern area name Tor di Quinto derives.

The praetorians are depicted in characteristic scale armour and with a typically ornate *signum* (standard) decorated with crowns (awards for bravery) and *imagines* (portraits) of Maxentius and Romulus, his deified son (**4**). Their shields carry a Hercules blazon, recalling the patron deity of Maximian and symbolizing Maxentius' dynastic right to rule.

Constantine's soldiers are from the *Divitenses* detachment of *legio II Italica*. The praetorians' *pila* (javelin) volley has failed to halt their *concursus* (advance); the legionaries pause to hurl their own javelins before drawing swords and charging to close quarters. The *Divitenses* are named after their base at Divitia on the Rhine. The yellow and red concentric circles on their shields follow a pattern later recorded for the unit in the Notitia Dignitatum (*Oc.* 5.4). The Christogram has been daubed over this (**5**).

THE BATTLE OF THE MILVIAN BRIDGE: A TENTATIVE RECONSTRUCTION

Having surveyed the principal literary and iconographic sources for the battle and considered the topographical and archaeological landscape of Tor di Quinto and the Pons Mulvius region, it is time to suggest a reconstruction of what might have happened at the battle of the Milvian Bridge.

Contrary to the report of Lactantius (*DMP* 44.9), the Milvian Bridge was broken in advance of Constantine's arrival in the *regio*. Considering its strategic importance (lying on the main route into Rome at the junction of the Viae Flaminia and Cassia, the *diverticulum* running over the high ground to the plain of Tor di Quinto, and the ancient Tiberina–Clodia route that followed the right bank of the Tiber down to Trans Tiberim), it is proposed here that, like Vitellius in AD 69 (Dio 64.191.2), Maxentius positioned a strong force at this point to counter any attempt by Constantine to advance down the Via Cassia, or the *diverticulum* from Tor di Quinto, and seize the bridge. The bridge's broken arches would hamper Constantine's advance on Rome, but only momentarily. His engineers could easily repair the superstructure (cf. Hdn. 8.4.1–5: huge wine barrels used to form pontoons to bridge the Sontius (Isonzo) in AD 238).

With the arches of the Milvian Bridge broken (as depicted on the frieze of the Arch of Constantine), Maxentius' engineers constructed a bridge of boats upstream (*Epit.* 40.7). It was not intended as a trap for Constantine but to convey part of Maxentius' army across river to Tor di Quinto, from where it marched up the Via Flaminia and mauled Constantine's vanguard when it tried to force the narrows at Saxa Rubra (Landmann 1913, 148; Lact. *DMP* 44.3; Aur. Vict. 40.23).

Despite the situation being little different to AD 307 when Severus and Galerius threatened Rome, the success at Saxa Rubra persuaded Maxentius to abandon his original plan of standing siege. On 26 October he decided to engage Constantine in open battle but, aware of the risk he was taking, moved his family out of the palace and into the relative safety of an anonymous house somewhere in Rome (*Pan. Lat.* 12(9).16.4). It may have been on the same day, or on the 27th as Lactantius reports (*DMP* 44.8), that Maxentius, the traditional Roman religionist, found a useful passage in the Sibylline Books concerning the destruction of an enemy of Rome (cf. Zos. 2.16.1). As the self-proclaimed *conservator* of Rome, charismatic and persuasive Maxentius could use the oracle to justify his decision to fight in the open field and his troops, having discovered at Saxa Rubra that Constantine's army was not invincible, would believe it.

Gilded ridge helmet with coloured glass ornaments from Berkasovo. Constantine wore a similar helmet at the battle of the Milvian Bridge, but his was adorned with real gems. (Jebulon)

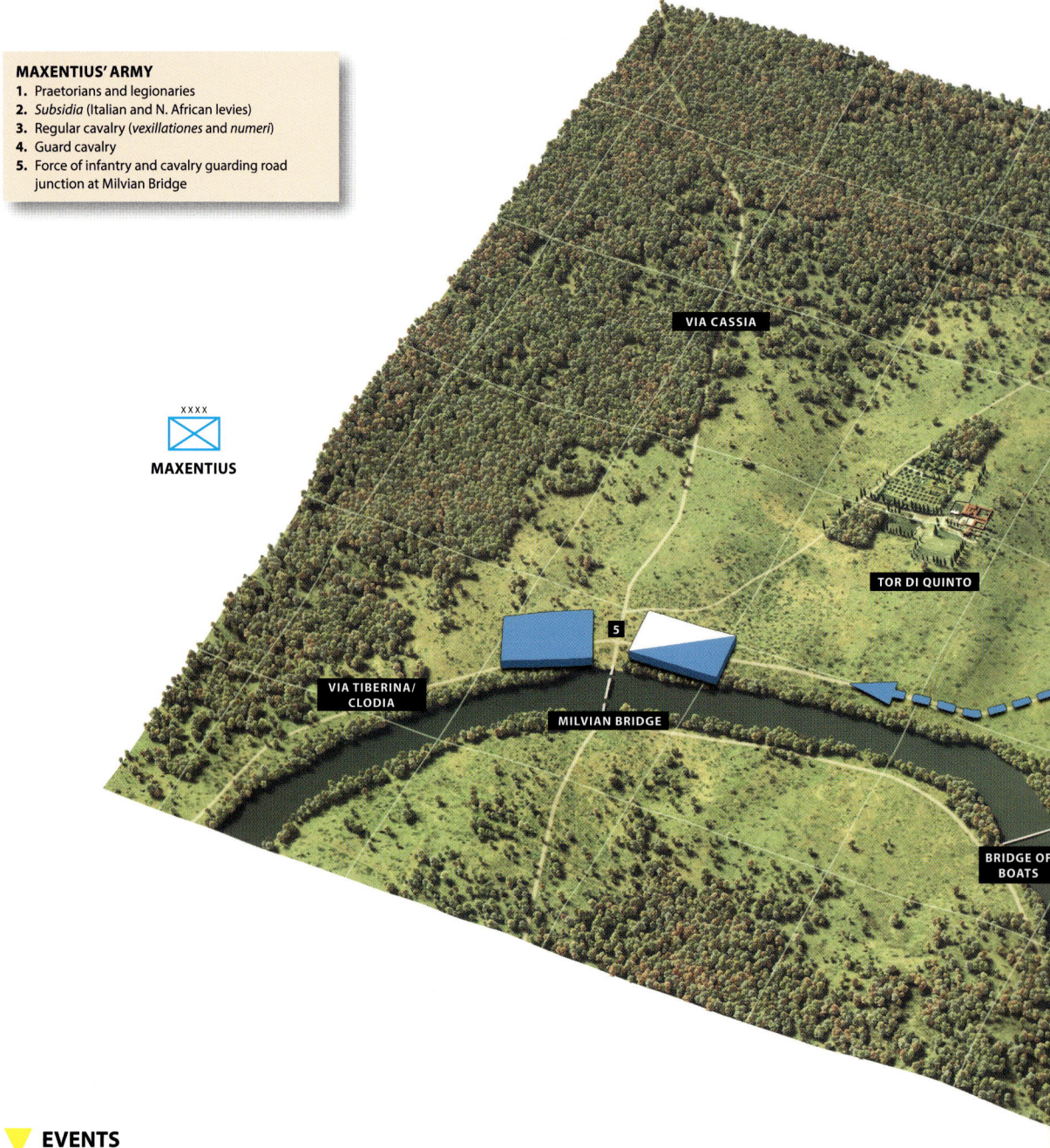

MAXENTIUS' ARMY
1. Praetorians and legionaries
2. *Subsidia* (Italian and N. African levies)
3. Regular cavalry (*vexillationes* and *numeri*)
4. Guard cavalry
5. Force of infantry and cavalry guarding road junction at Milvian Bridge

EVENTS

1. Constantine sends his second cavalry division to reinforce the first and the resistance of the Maxentian cavalry collapses.

2. The horsemen flee towards the bridge of boats or down the Via Flaminia in the direction of the Milvian Bridge.

3. Maxentius, retreating with the cavalry guard, attempts to ford the Tiber upstream of the bridge of boats.

4. The right flank and rear of the Maxentian infantry formation is now exposed and the *subsidia* panic and join the cavalry in flight.

THE ROUT BEGINS

Maxentius' cavalry collapses and flees, exposing the flank of his infantry. The levies at the rear of the infantry formation panic and join the cavalry in flight.

Note: Gridlines are shown at intervals of 500m

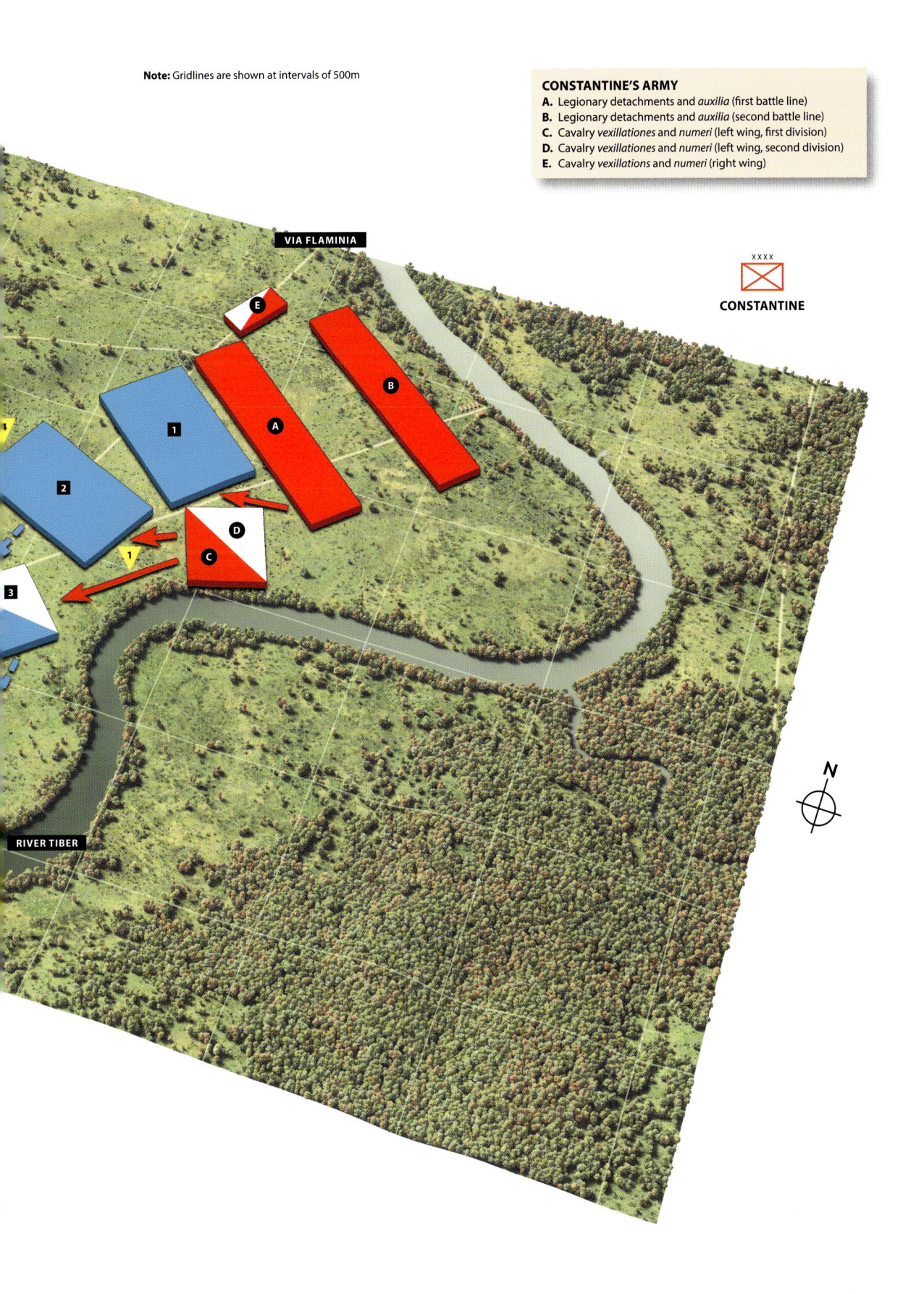

CONSTANTINE'S ARMY
A. Legionary detachments and *auxilia* (first battle line)
B. Legionary detachments and *auxilia* (second battle line)
C. Cavalry *vexillationes* and *numeri* (left wing, first division)
D. Cavalry *vexillationes* and *numeri* (left wing, second division)
E. Cavalry *vexillations* and *numeri* (right wing)

VIA FLAMINIA

CONSTANTINE

RIVER TIBER

By 27 October, Constantine had marched from Saxa Rubra to the northern part of the plain of Tor di Quinto. The progress of his army down the narrow strip of land between the Tiber and the tufa cliffs was likely slow and cautious. Constantine's vanguard was perhaps harassed by Maxentian light troops such as the Mauri javelineers and mounted *lanciarii*, but there was no attempt to bring the war to a conclusion in the region of what is now Grottarossa. After the victory at Saxa Rubra the bulk of Maxentius' army had crossed back over the Tiber, but it did not necessarily return to Rome. There was probably already a Maxentian camp at the southern end of the bridge of boats in the old estate of the Villa of the Auditorium between the left bank of the Tiber and the Parioli Hills. Part of the Maxentian force would have remained on Tor di Quinto to guard the north end of the bridge

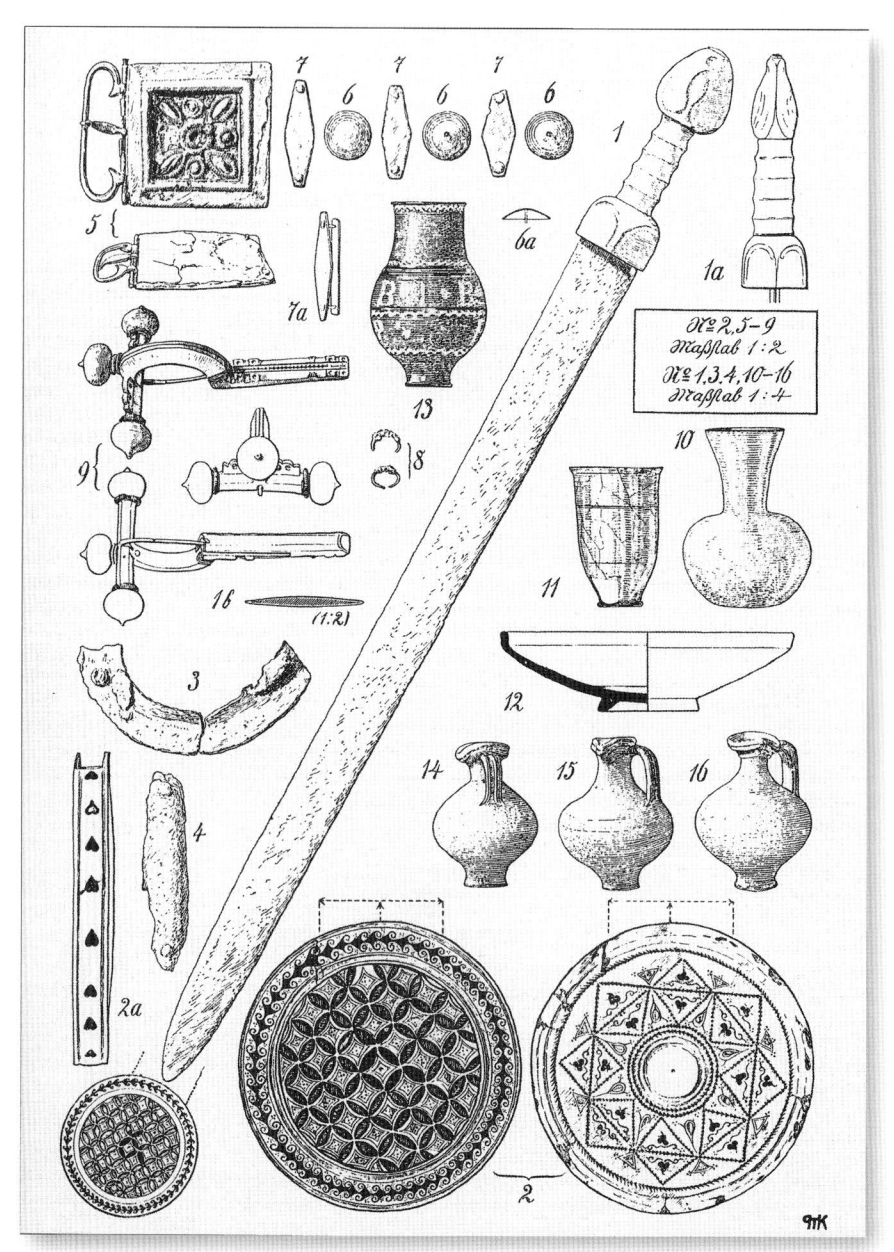

Sword of the late 3rd century AD from Cologne, typical of the type used at the Milvian Bridge in AD 312. (RHC Archive)

of boats (note Lact. *DMP* 44.6 for the presence of Maxentius' men on the right bank of the Tiber while he was still in Rome).

Both Constantine and Maxentius recognized that the plain of Tor di Quinto was big enough to fight an engagement but there was little scope for extended battle lines and outflanking manoeuvres. The field was suited to a head-on and, hopefully, decisive encounter. Therefore Maxentius allowed Constantine to bivouac at the head of the plain, and Constantine left Maxentius' bridgeheads unmolested.

Constantine began the war with somewhat less than 40,000 men – the most he believed could be withdrawn from his territory without compromising its security. He suffered losses at Verona but also gained a large number of captives. It is possible that he enrolled some into his field army but, considering Maxentius' talent for undermining the loyalty of the soldiers of his opponents, it is doubtful that Constantine would have taken such a risk. It is more likely that they were distributed among the units on Constantine's eventful German frontier (cf. *Pan. Lat.* 12(9).21.2–3). While still in northern Italy, Constantine may have received some reinforcements from his regulars in Gaul and Germany, but prior to invading Central Italy he had to establish strong garrisons in those cities which he had conquered from Maxentius. Civilian uprisings were most unlikely, but a sudden invasion by Licinius was possible. The field army Constantine led to the threshold of Rome was, in the opinion of the present writer, in the region of 20,000–25,000 men. He would have considered this an adequate force – if Maxentius could be drawn out of Rome. Fourteen years earlier, Constantine was a tribune in a similarly sized Roman army that had vanquished the Persians in battle in Armenia and then captured Ctesiphon (Fest. *Brev*. 25).

The defeats of his field armies at Augusta Taurinorum, Brixia and Verona, and the loss of his major garrisons at Segusio, Verona, Aquileia and Mutina, had greatly diminished Maxentius' forces. Of the 100,000 he could muster at the start of the war (the regulars he had filched from Severus and Galerius and his recently conscripted Italians and Africans), at least two-thirds had been killed, captured or surrendered. By late October, his available forces may have amounted to no more than 25,000. A large number of veterans, including some praetorians and other guardsmen, would have been lost with Ruricius Pompeianus at Verona, but Maxentius had clearly retained the bulk of the Praetorian Guard at Rome and it formed the core of his army, probably over 8,000 men (i.e. less a cohort or vexillation given to Pompeianus), and would have included those men who had known victory under Maximian and more recently with Volusianus and Zenas in Africa.

On the evening of 27 October, Constantine's army camped in the northern part of Tor di Quinto. During the night, the emperor had his famous dream instructing him to mark the Christogram, the heavenly sign of God, on the shields of his soldiers (Lact. *DMP* 44.5). This was doubtless confirmed as a genuine message from God by Ossius, the bishop of Corduba (Cordova) and member of Constantine's campaign entourage (Seeck 1921, 495 on Euseb. *HE* 10.6.2). Encouraged by this demonstration of divine support, Constantine offered battle on the morning of 28 October. Maxentius accepted and crossed the bridge of boats without any interference from Constantine's forces (Lact. *DMP* 44.6).

The anonymous orator of AD 313 and Nazarius emphasize Maxentius' appalling position on the plain, with the Tiber to the rear of his men, leaving

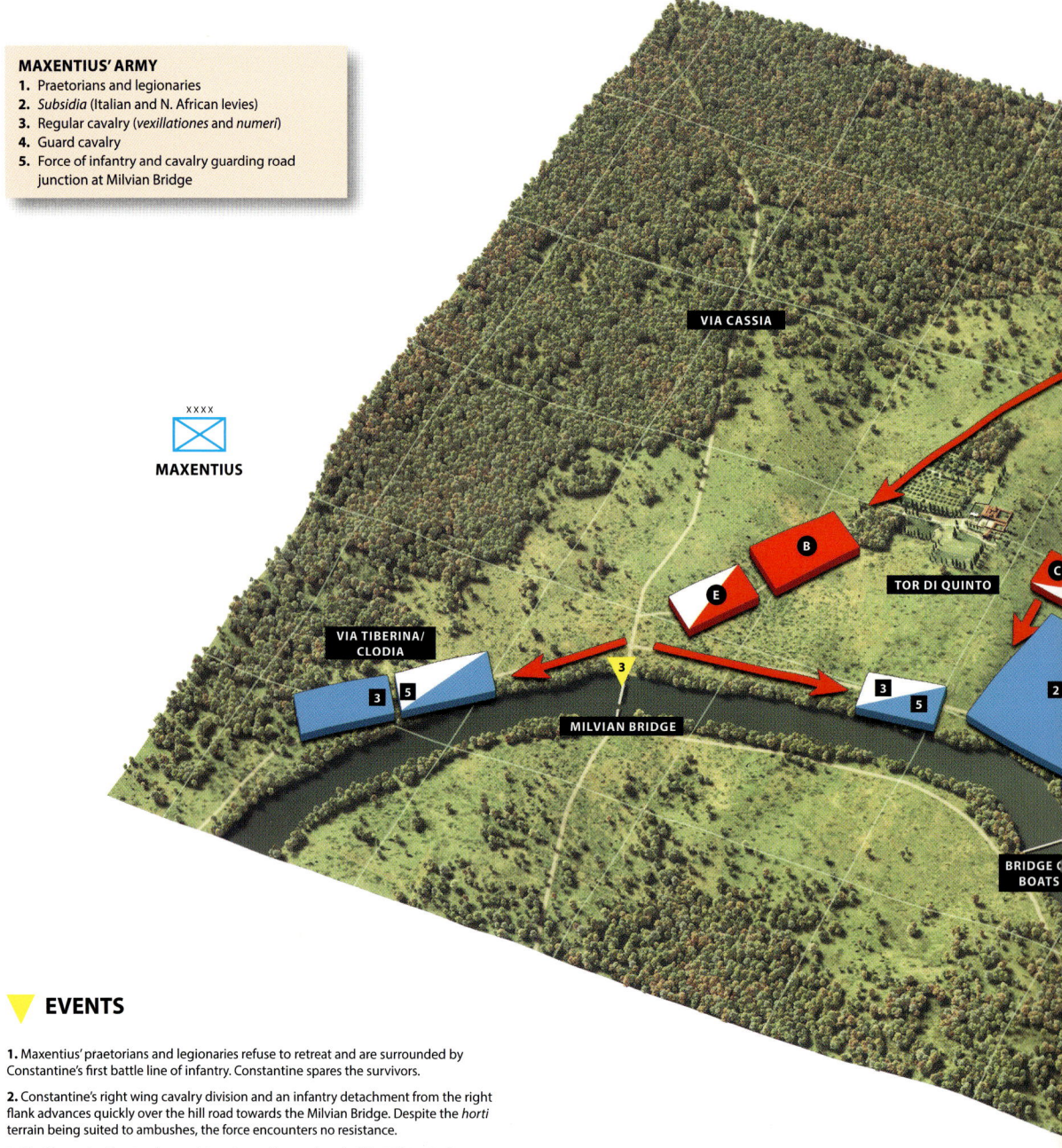

MAXENTIUS' ARMY
1. Praetorians and legionaries
2. *Subsidia* (Italian and N. African levies)
3. Regular cavalry (*vexillationes* and *numeri*)
4. Guard cavalry
5. Force of infantry and cavalry guarding road junction at Milvian Bridge

▼ **EVENTS**

1. Maxentius' praetorians and legionaries refuse to retreat and are surrounded by Constantine's first battle line of infantry. Constantine spares the survivors.

2. Constantine's right wing cavalry division and an infantry detachment from the right flank advances quickly over the hill road towards the Milvian Bridge. Despite the *horti* terrain being suited to ambushes, the force encounters no resistance.

3. The Maxentian force at the road junction at the north end of the Milvian Bridge (positioned to counter any attempt by a Constantinian detachment to circle round the rear of Maxentius' main army by the Tor di Quinto hill road or the Via Cassia) is already in flight, having been infected by the panic of the cavalry defeated on the plain. The Maxentians flee down the Via Tiberina/Clodia towards the Trans Tiberim suburb of Rome, or attempt to reach the bridge of boats by the Via Flaminia. They are pursued in both directions by Constantine's cavalry and the infantry detachment.

4. Maxentius' forces on the plain are pursued by Constantine's cavalry divisions and his second battle line of infantry. Most Maxentians flee to the bridge of boats, but it becomes overloaded and breaks up. The other fugitives are either cut down or are forced into the Tiber to drown alongside Maxentius and his guardsmen.

THE ROUT COMPLETE

The praetorians and legionaries refuse to retreat and are surrounded. The rest of Maxentius' army is pursued towards the Tiber. The bridge of boats collapses under the weight of the fugitives. Maxentius drowns in the river.

Note: Gridlines are shown at intervals of 500m

CONSTANTINE'S ARMY
A. Legionary detachments and *auxilia* (first battle line)
B. Legionary detachments and *auxilia* (second battle line)
C. Cavalry *vexillationes* and *numeri* (left wing, first division)
D. Cavalry *vexillationes* and *numeri* (left wing, second division)
E. Cavalry *vexillations* and *numeri* (right wing)

VIA FLAMINIA

CONSTANTINE

RIVER TIBER

no room to manoeuvre or any line of retreat (*Pan. Lat.* 12(9).16.3; 4(10).28.1, 4). However, Constantine's army would also have the river to its back, something that would have encouraged Maxentius and his commanders. It is proposed here that, because of the limited area of the plain, Constantine's army was arrayed in a *duplex acies* (cf. his initial deployment at Verona: *Pan. Lat.* 12(9).9.1). He stationed the bulk of his cavalry on the left wing, while the remainder was positioned on the Via Flaminia on the right wing to react to any attempt by Maxentius to send a force down the *diverticulum* that ran over the high ground to attack the flank or rear of Constantine's formation.

It must have taken some time for Maxentius' army to cross the Tiber and deploy into its battle formation. The space available to Maxentius at the southern end of Tor di Quinto was limited and not suited to a typical linear formation. He instead formed his infantry into an *agmen quadratum*, a defensive square formation. The praetorians and legionary veterans would have been in the leading division, with the Italian and African conscripts forming a second, or reserve division of *subsidia* (*Pan. Lat.* 4(10).28.4–5). The left flank of the *agmen quadratum* was secured by the steep hills rising to the west of the plain. Maxentius' cavalry, again in two divisions, formed on the open ground between the right flank of the infantry and the bank of the Tiber (Zos. 2.16.4 for Maxentius' second force of cavalry).

When Maxentius' army advanced to the outcrop on which the Torre di Quinto was built, Constantine launched his assault. Leading his first division of cavalry, the splendidly armoured emperor smashed into Maxentius' leading squadrons and immediately routed them (*Pan. Lat.* 4(10).29.5–6; Zos. 2.16.2). Constantine then gave the signal for his legionary vexillations and regiments of *auxilia* to charge the *agmen quadratum* (*Pan. Lat.* 4(10).29.3). But the praetorians and other Maxentian veterans would give no ground (Zos. 2.16.3; *Pan. Lat.* 12(9).17.1). With the cavalry crumbling, the right flank of the *agmen quadratum* was vulnerable, but the Maxentian cavalry were steadied by reinforcements, which included Maxentius and his guardsmen (Zos. 2.16.4; Euseb. *HE* 9.9.5).

Maxentius and his guardsmen retrieved the situation only momentarily. The divinely inspired Constantine would not be denied the victory he had been promised and pressed his attack. Maxentius' cavalry collapsed. There were no more reserves and the bulk of the horsemen turned and fled for the bridge of boats or down the Via Flaminia in the direction of the Milvian Bridge and Trans Tiberim. Constantine's troopers were in hot pursuit and Maxentius was now exposed. His guardsmen steered him away from the growing crush at the north end of the bridge of boats or the bottleneck where the Via Flaminia turns the bend at Torre Lazzaroni and is constrained between the high ground and the Tiber. They instead attempted to swim the Tiber upstream of the bridge (*Pan. Lat.* 12(9).17.1), aiming perhaps for what is now Acqua Acetosa on the opposite bank, which would allow access to the Via Salaria Vetus and escape to Rome. However, the river is notoriously swift of current. 'The Tiber, as low down as Rome, retains many of the characteristics of the mountain torrent. Even when the river is low, the current is strong' (Smith 1877, 38). It may be that the Tiber was swollen by autumn rains in October AD 312 (Seeck 1921, 133). Antonius Primus' cavalry successfully negotiated the Tiber in the rainy December of AD 69, but Maxentius and his guardsmen had no time to plan their crossing. Pursued by Constantine's cavalry, they plunged into the Tiber in a mad rush and 'sank as lead into the mighty waters' (Euseb. *HE* 9.9.7).

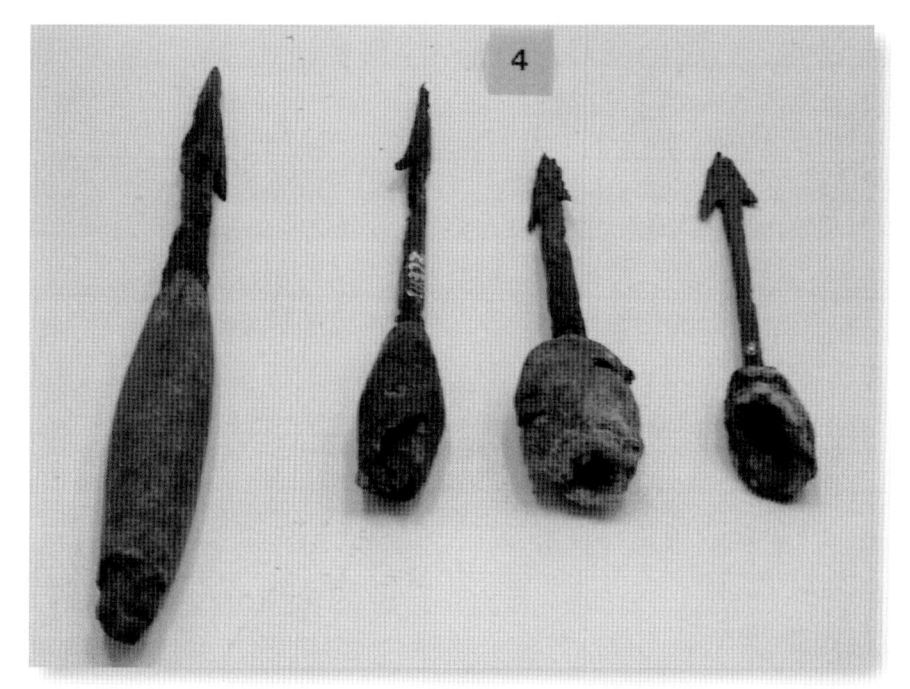

Plumbatae. The combatants at the Milvian Bridge would have been bombarded throughout the battle with barbed, lead-weighted missiles like these. (Florian Himmler)

Maxentius' Italian and African levies had played no active part in the battle. They merely added bulk to the *agmen quadratum*. When the cavalry were defeated the flank and rear of the *agmen quadratum* were exposed. At the sight of Maxentius himself in flight, the levies broke and joined the chaotic retreat (Zos. 2.16.3–4; Lact. *DMP* 44.9). The proud praetorians, however, did not join the flight (*Pan. Lat.* 12(9).17.1). They continued to fight and were surrounded by the first line of Constantine's *duplex acies*.

With the bulk of Maxentius' army in flight, Constantine now sent part of his army, namely the cavalry he had positioned on his right flank on the Via Flaminia and infantry from the second line of the *duplex acies*, over the *diverticulum* running through the *horti* of Ovid. That Constantine used this road to access the Via Cassia and seize the north end of the Milvian Bridge, is suggested by the frieze on the Arch of Constantine (see **no. 3**, above).

The *horti* of Ovid would have been the perfect place for Maxentius to have planted light troops to harass any attempt made by Constantine to traverse the *diverticulum*. When Hannibal led an army to the outskirts of Rome in 211 BC, the consuls ordered 1,200 Numidian light troops to prepare to defend the Esquiline region of the city: 'no troops would be better suited to fighting in land consisting of hollows, of buildings set in *horti*, or amongst tombs and a maze of sunken lanes' (Liv. 26.10.5–6). The Numidians were not needed, for Hannibal withdrew. In AD 69, the Vitellian defenders of Rome slowed the Flavian advance in the Gardens of Sallust by 'climbing on top of the walls that surrounded the gardens, [where they] blocked their opponents' approach with a shower of stones and *pila* until, late in the day, they were finally surrounded' (Tac. *Hist.* 3.82). But with Constantine camped at the north of Tor di Quinto and able to access the *horti* by the *diverticulum* or the valley of the Acquatraversa, it may be that be that Maxentius preferred not to risk his own men in the maze of walls and lanes and instead concentrated them at the road junction at the north end of the Milvian Bridge. Similarly, Constantine would have been wary of any traps,

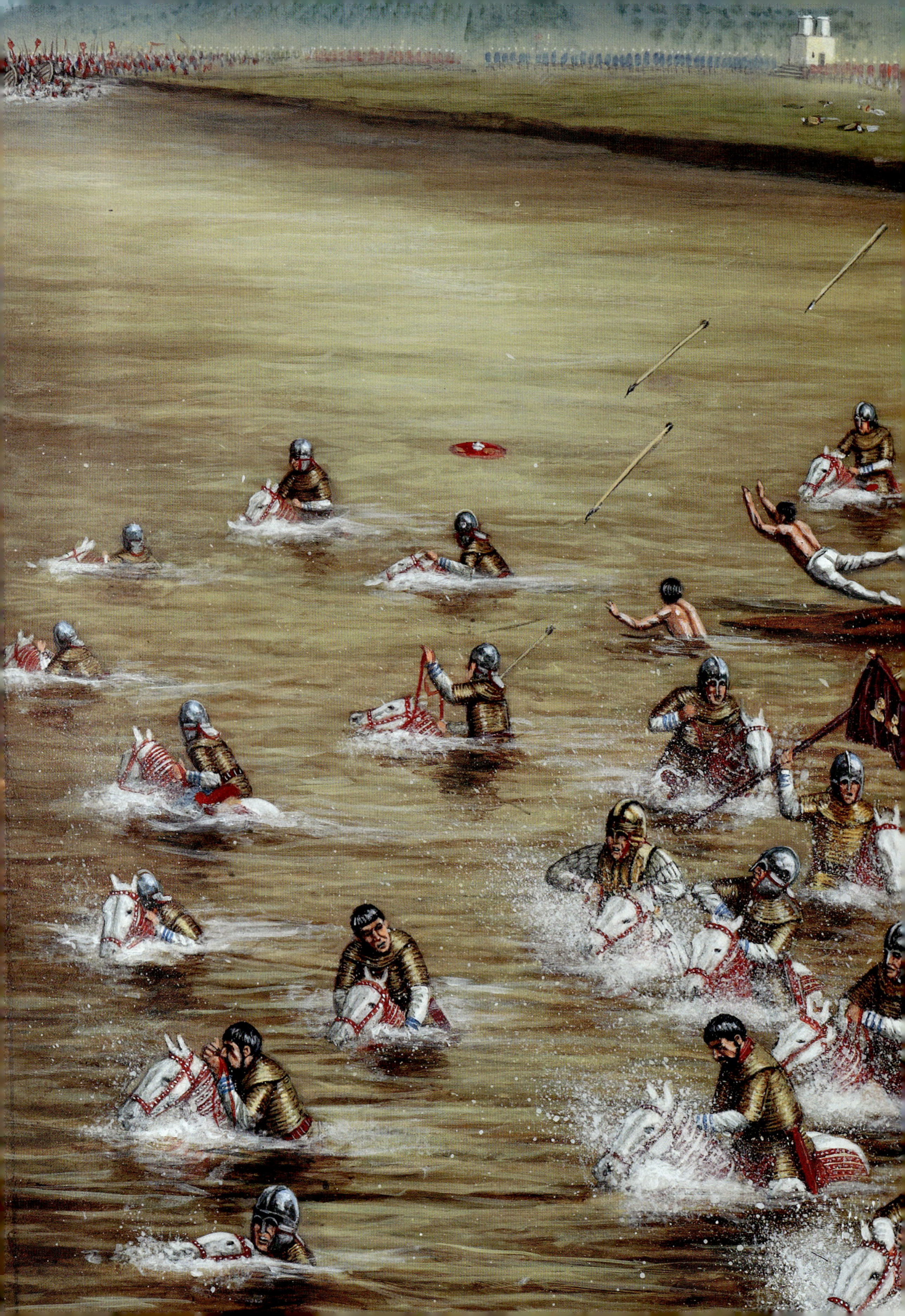

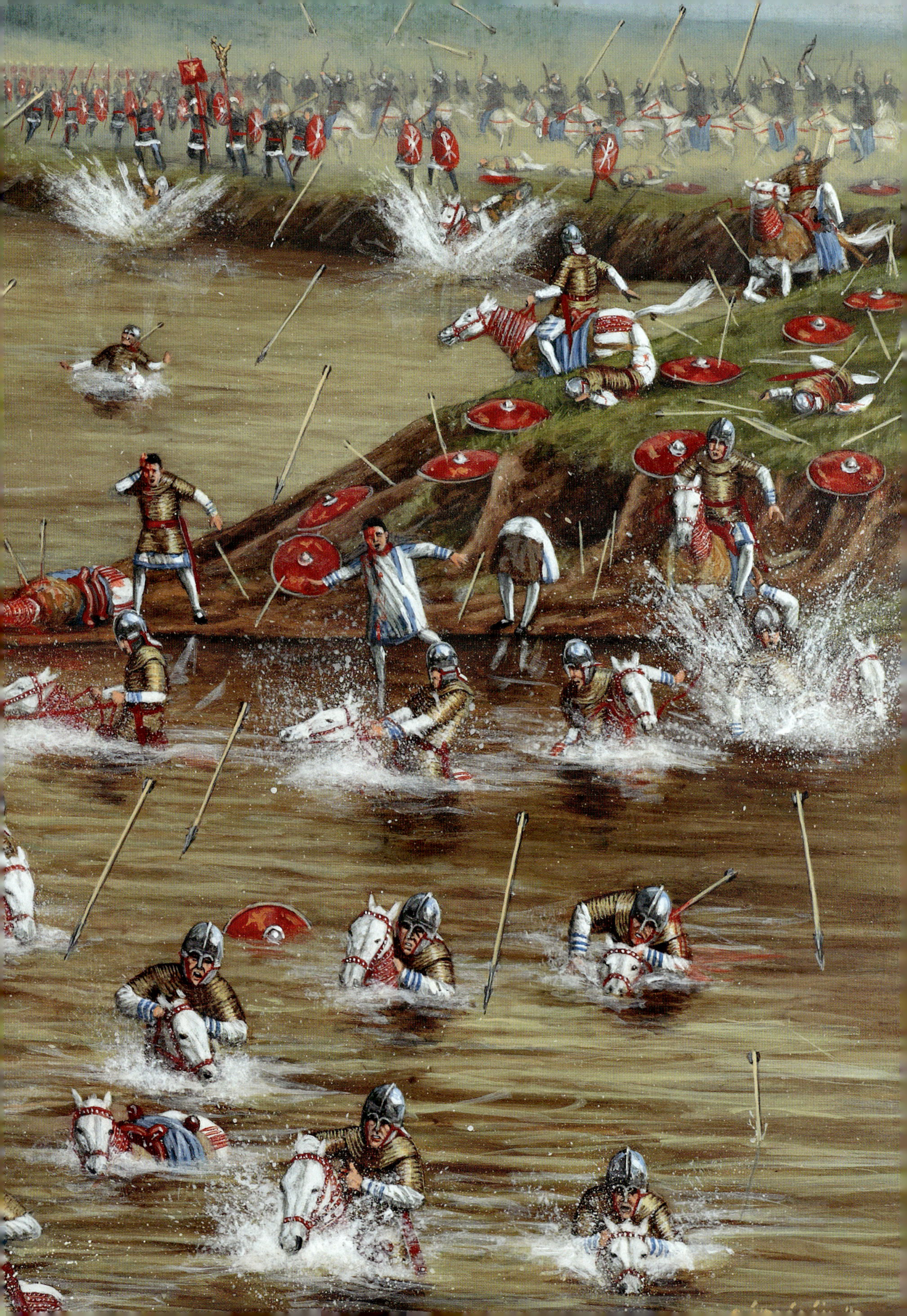

THE ROUT (PP. 82–83)

With the bridge of boats already overcrowded with fugitives, Maxentius and his *equites singulares* attempt to swim the Tiber and gain the opposite bank at what is now Acqua Acetosa (**1**). However, the emperor and his guardsmen are bombarded with missiles by their Constantinian pursuers and the current of the river, swollen by autumn rains, is too strong (**2**). Maxentius and his comrades will drown, as will the soldiers attempting to escape by the bridge of boats, which is about to collapse.

The background gives an impression of the developed landscape of the Pons Mulvius *regio* of this part of the Roman *suburbium*. The imposing villa of Ovid stands on the hill lying between the Via Cassia and Via Flaminia, and is surrounded by *horti* (decorative and market gardens). *Horti* were divided by high walls and linked by sunken lanes and were difficult places in which to fight, but Constantine may have sent a division over the hill to attack a Maxentian force posted at the north end of the Milvian Bridge.

On the plain below, a large and unusual double drum mausoleum is built beside the Via Flaminia (**3**). In fact, the course of the road from the Milvian Bridge to the north end of Tor di Quinto was lined with memorials to the dead.

obstructions or ambushes Maxentius's troops might have placed in the *horti* prior to returning to their positions at the Pons Mulvius and the north end of the bridge of boats. Thus on 28 October, when Constantine's men finally entered the *horti*, they found them undefended and moved swiftly along the *diverticulum* to the Via Cassia and Milvian Bridge, where they swiftly dislodged the garrison (it was perhaps already in flight) and intercepted the fugitives coming down the Via Flaminia from Tor di Quinto.

ROUT

The battle of the Milvian Bridge was hard fought (*Lact. DMP* 44.6, 9; cf. Zos. 2.16.3), but the battle was of notably short duration (*Pan. Lat.* 4(10).30.2) and was lost for Maxentius when his cavalry collapsed and he was caught up in its panicked flight (Zos. 2.16.4). The crossing of the Tiber and the deployment of Maxentius' army into the *agmen quadratum* would have taken hours, whereas the actual fighting was probably over in less than an hour.

The first Maxentians to reach the bridge of boats presumably managed to cross the Tiber and headed for Rome or beyond, but the bridge, which was probably some 125–150m in length, was soon overloaded and collapsed under the mass of fugitives. Some of the boats sank and men and horses were swept downstream with the debris of the superstructure (Euseb. *HE* 9.9.7; Zos. 2.16.4). It is not known how many drowned in this disaster, or with Maxentius or other groups that attempted to swim the river, but the Tiber became so clogged with corpses that its current was slowed. The Maxentians stranded at the southern end of Tor di Quinto, or trapped on the Via Flaminia between the Milvian Bridge and the plain were slaughtered by Constantine's soldiers and the right bank of the Tiber was covered with an unbroken line of dead (*Pan. Lat.* 12(9).17.2; 4(10).30.1).

Detail of the Milvian Bridge Frieze on the Arch of Constantine. Constantine's victorious soldiers force Maxentian cavalry into the swirling waters of the Tiber. (Florian Himmler)

AFTERMATH

PRAETORIANS AND HORSE GUARDS

Interestingly, the praetorians (and perhaps also a number of legionary veterans) who had determined on a last stand on the plain were not killed to a man. Perhaps Constantine was moved by their courage and intervened to prevent a massacre. Constantine certainly pardoned the survivors and distributed them among the garrisons on his German frontier where, as early as AD 313, their fighting prowess against the barbarian enemies of the Empire was noted (*Pan. Lat.* 12(9).21.2–3). But these men were praetorians no longer. Constantine's mercy went only so far.

In AD 193, Septimius Severus dishonourably discharged every soldier in the Praetorian Guard for their connivance in the assassination of the emperor Pertinax and the elevation of Didius Julianus, but he immediately re-established the Guard with recruits drawn from his own legions (Dio

Constantine built the Lateran Basilica over the New Fort of the *equites singulares*, but parts of the fort, including barracks and its finely decorated headquarters, survive amid the foundations of the church. (Lalupa)

74.2.4–6). As we have seen, Constantine certainly had guardsmen in his army, some of whom originally served in the Praetorian Guard, but he had no wish to maintain such a powerful and potentially dangerous military institution. The cohorts of the Praetorian Guard and the *numeri* of the *equites singulares Augusti* were formally dissolved (Aur. Vict. 40.25). Victor also states that the guardsmen were stripped of their arms and military garments; they were therefore dishonourably discharged from the army. We have noted, however, that the ex-praetorians were allowed to continue soldiering. Victor may be repeating the punishment doled out by Severus to the praetorians in AD 193, but, considering the destruction wrought by Constantine on the forts and memorials of the horse guardsmen (below), it seems that Victor accurately records the fate of the few surviving *equites singulares*; the disgraceful sentence of dishonourable discharge was a potent punishment in a society obsessed with honour and rank. But Victor erroneously assumed that the punishment also extended to the praetorians.

The fortresses of the guardsmen, the mighty Castra Praetoria and the Old and New Forts of the Horse Guard, were demolished (Zos. 2.17.2). The north, east and south walls of the Castra Praetoria had been incorporated into Aurelian's Wall of Rome and so still survive, but the forts of the Horse Guard, both within the circuit of the wall, were destroyed. Churches honouring the God who had inspired Constantine to victory at the Milvian Bridge were promptly built over the sites of the New Fort (the Basilica of St John Lateran) and the horse guardsmen's principal burial ground on the Via Labicana (Basilica of Saints Marcellinus and Peter) (*Lib. Pont.* 34.26–27; Barnes 2011, 84–89). Such was Constantine's ire with the *equites singulares*, perhaps because the horsemen had temporarily stemmed his cavalry assault and attempted to extricate Maxentius from the field, that he had the tombstones of their comrades in the Via Labicana cemetery smashed and used the rubble as foundations for the grand basilica church (Speidel 1994a, 156–157; 1994b, 1–3).

Despite his clemency towards the praetorian survivors of the Milvian Bridge, Constantine could not forgive their elevation of Maxentius, and he also targeted their cemeteries for building materials and redevelopment. The tombstones of 1st- and 2nd-century date that lined the Via Flaminia were dug up and used to repair the road (Rossi 2012, 306–307). The site of the main praetorian cemetery on the Via Nomentana was later gifted by Constantine to his daughter Constantina (sometimes erroneously called Constantia) for her mausoleum complex and the establishment of the basilica of St Agnes (*Lib. Pont.* 34.23; Barnes 2011, 151). It is ironic, then, that the Arch of Constantine, which is liberally decorated with *spolia* depicting the Praetorian Guard in attendance on Trajan and Marcus Aurelius (whose features were re-cut to resemble Constantine), acts as a great memorial to the guardsmen.

A huge imperial mausoleum, now known as Tor Pignattara, forms part of the Saints Marcellinus and Peter complex. It was built for Constantine, but Helena, who died *c.* AD 328, was interred there instead. Her huge sarcophagus of red porphyry was originally intended for Constantine and is decorated with scenes of triumphant Roman horsemen riding down captives, some of whom are bound. It has been suggested that the captives represent the *equites singulares* defeated at the Milvian Bridge (Speidel 1994a, 157), but the bare-chested and bearded figures are barbarians. Rather than glorify a victory over fellow-citizens (even Constantine admitted that Maxentius' followers had been deceived and led astray by the tyrant: *Oratio* 22), the sarcophagus commemorated Constantine's labours in the defence of the Roman Empire and his role as *propagator*, an extender, of its frontiers (cf. *ILS* 699).

CONSTANTINE ENTERS ROME

Maxentius' body was discovered the day after the battle of the Milvian Bridge. Perhaps because of all the corpses in the river and the wreckage of the bridge of boats, it was not carried far downstream and was easily identified by its rich armour and imperial garments.

The Roman calendar records Constantine's *evictio tyranni*, 'the eviction of the tyrant', on 28 October, and his *adventus* into Rome on the 29th (*CIL* I² p. 274). The *adventus* was the ceremonial entry into the city by an emperor returning from campaign. The frieze on the east side of the Arch of Constantine depicts the *adventus*. Constantine, swathed in his general's cloak, rides into the city on a *quadriga*, a four-wheeled carriage; the goddess Victory drives the team of four horses, and bodyguards look on warily as the carriage passes by. One of them wears a neck torque, a military decoration for valour. Constantine would have distributed such awards the morning after the battle (cf. Porfyrius 6.26–28; Amm. Marc. 24.6.15). The carriage is preceded by ranks of smartly marching infantry and a troop of cavalry trots along with the long tails of their dragon standards streaming above. The following scenes of the frieze, on the north face of the Arch, show Constantine addressing the newly liberated Senate and people of Rome in the Forum and then distributing bread to the grateful citizens.

The anonymous orator of AD 313 and Nazarius (who may have witnessed the procession) describe Constantine's entry into Rome more in terms of a *triumphus* than an *adventus* (*Pan Lat.* 12(9).18.3–19.3; 4(10).31.4–32.6). The triumph was distinguished from the *adventus* by the display of captives and trophies in the procession, by the soldiers' singing of ribald and abusive songs, and by a slave who rode in the four-horse chariot of the *triumphator*

Constantine's *adventus* into Rome. The goddess Victory drives the emperor's carriage and a *torquatus* bodyguard looks on. (R. Martel)

to remind him he was not a conquering god but merely a mortal man. According to the panegyrists, Maxentius' head was impaled on a spear and carried before Constantine's carriage. Abuse was hurled at the head and the soldier carrying the spear, 'since he suffered the deserts of another's head' (*ibid.* 12(9).18.3). However, unlike conquering generals of old, the newly Christian Constantine did not process to the Capitol and sacrifice to Jupiter.

Maxentius' severed head demonstrated to the Romans that he was dead; it was then sent to Africa as proof of Constantine's victory. It is not known what happened to Valeria Maximilla and Maxentius' unnamed son. Valeria was young enough to remarry and her status as the daughter of a senior emperor might attract suitors who would use her to legitimize their own imperial aspirations. Despite the false confession Constantine extracted from the empress Eutropia (his mother-in-law) about Maxentius being the bastard of a Syrian (*Origo* 4.12), as the grandson of two senior emperors, the nameless boy had a hereditary claim to rule that Constantine could not tolerate. The boy and Valeria were probably done away with. Licinius' purge of all members of Diocletian's and Galerius' families in AD 313 (Lact. *DMP* 50–51) and Constantine's execution of Crispus, Fausta and Licinius junior in AD 326 (Eutrop. 10.6) are indicative of the ruthlessness of the age.

The mother of Licinius junior was Constantia, the half-sister of Constantine. She married Licinius at Mediolanum in February AD 313. Constantine, having been made senior Augustus by a Senate eager to ingratiate itself with the conqueror (Lact. *DMP* 44.9), impressed on his new brother-in-law and effective subordinate that Christianity was to be tolerated in the eastern dioceses of the empire; the property of the Church was to be returned and it would be allowed to flourish. This resulted in the so-called Edict of Milan (Euseb. *HE* 10.5.2–14). The opportunity to remove Maximinus, who had resumed the persecution of the Christians, presented itself at the same time. Furious at being usurped as senior Augustus and still hungering for his uncle's European territories, Maximinus invaded Thrace but Licinius raced eastwards and routed him at Campus Ergenus on 30 April AD 313. Maximinus committed suicide soon after. Relations between Constantine and Licinius quickly deteriorated. War flared up in AD 316–17 and Licinius lost all of his European possessions except for Thrace. A second war, in AD 324, saw his total defeat and in AD 325 he was executed. Constantine, favourite of Apollo and Sol and warrior of Christ, had conquered all.

Unpublished milestone now at Brindisi. The inscription describes Constantine as 'Liberator of the Roman state'. (Duncan B. Campbell)

THE BATTLEFIELD TODAY

The battlefield of Tor di Quinto, the high ground between the Via Cassia and the Via Flaminia where Ovid once tended his gardens, and the banks of the Tiber on either side of the Pons Mulvius (Ponte Milvio) are now highly developed. The modern visitor is greeted by major roads, apartment blocks, sporting and military facilities including, aptly, the hippodrome of the riding school of the Italian Army where, it has been proposed in the preceding pages, the cavalry of Constantine and Maxentius clashed. The hippodrome, and what remains of the open ground to the east and north, is best viewed from the cycle path that follows the Tiber from Ponte Milvio to modern Saxa Rubra, just south of Labaro.

Parco di Tor di Quinto is located at the south of the plain. It was here that, having crossed the river using the bridge of boats, the army of Maxentius may have formed into an *agmen quadratum*. If the modern visitor to the park

The Milvian Bridge, known today as the Ponte Milvio, remains an impressive monument, but the modern visitor will find little else to evoke the landscape of AD 312. (P. Ferri)

looks to the west, he or she can appreciate the size and sheerness of the cliffs that secured the left flank of Maxentius' battle formation.

To get a sense of the scale of the plain of Tor di Quinto and its setting between the high ground and the bend of the river, it is necessary to cross the Tiber and head for the elevated points of Villa Glori or Monte Antenne (ancient Antemnae) in Villa Ada. However, views are limited because of the thick tree cover.

The Milvian Bridge itself remains an impressive monument. It was extensively rebuilt in the 15th and 19th centuries, but the four central arches date from 109 BC when the original Pons Mulvius (first attested in 207 BC) was reconstructed by Aemilius Scaurus.

For a site Constantine passed through immediately before the fighting at Saxa Rubra and the battle of the Milvian Bridge, and that still evokes the ancient Roman landscape and retains the charm of the Campagna, the reader is advised to seek out the Arch of Malborghetto near the 13th milestone of the Via Flaminia.

Looking west across Parco di Tor di Quinto to the high ground of the gardens of Ovid, now covered in modern apartment blocks. (Andyversus)

BIBLIOGRAPHY

Adams, J. N. & Brennan, P. M., 'The Text at Lactantius, *De Mortibus Persecutorum* 44.2, and Some Epigraphic Evidence for Italian Recruits' in *Zeitschrift für Papyrologie und Epigrafik* 84 (1990), 183–186

Alföldi, A., 'Cornuti: A Teutonic Contingent in the Service of Constantine the Great and Its Decisive Role in the Battle at the Milvian Bridge' in *Dumbarton Oaks Papers* 13 (1959), 169–183

Ashby, T. & Fell, R. A. L., 'The Via Flaminia' in *Journal of Roman Studies* 11 (1921), 125–190

Barnes, T., *Constantine and Eusebius*, Cambridge, Mass. & London: 1981

Barnes, T., *Constantine: Dynasty, Religion and Power in the Later Roman Empire*, Oxford: 2011

Casey, J., *Carausius and Allectus: The British Usurpers*, London: 1994

Christodoulou, D. N., 'Galerius, Gamzigrad and the Fifth Macedonian Legion' in *Journal of Roman Archaeology* 15 (2002), 275–281

Costa, G., 'La battaglia di Costantino a Ponte Milvio' in *Bilychnis* 2 (1913), 197–208

Duncan-Jones, R. P., 'Pay and Numbers in Diocletian's Army' in *Structure and Scale in the Roman Economy*, Cambridge: 1990, 105–117

Franzoni, C., *Habitus atque Habitudo Militis*, Rome: 1987

Frothingham, A. L. 'The Roman Territorial Arch' in *American Journal of Archaeology* 19 (1915), 155–174

Groag, E., 'Maxentius', *Realencyclopädie der klassischen Altertumswissenschaft* 14.2 (1930), 2417–2484

Grosse, G., *Römische Militärgeschichte von Gallienus bis zum Beginn der byzantinischen Themenverfassung*, Berlin: 1920

Grossi-Gondi, F., 'La battaglia di Costantino Magno a "Saxa Rubra"' in *Civiltà Cattolica* 63.4 (1912), 385–403

Hanel, N. & Verstegen, U., 'The Bridgehead Fort at Cologne-Deutz (Divitia) on the right bank of the Rhine' in *LIMES* XX, Madrid: 2009, 749–756

Hoffmann, D., *Das spätrömische Bewegungsheer und die Notitia Dignitatum*, Düsseldorf: 1969

Jones, A. H. M., *The Later Roman Empire 284–602*, Oxford: 1964

Kuhoff, W., 'Ein Mythos in der römischen Geschichte: Der Sieg Konstantins des Großen über Maxentius vor den Toren Roms am 28. Oktober 312 n. Chr.' in *Chiron* 21 (1991), 127–174

Kuhoff, W., 'Die Schlacht an der Milvische Brücke – Ein Ereignis von weltgeschichtlicher Tragweite' in K. Ehling & G. Weber (eds), *Konstantin der Grosse: Zwischen Sol und Christus*, Darmstadt: 2011

Landmann, K. von, 'Konstantin der Grosse als Feldherr' in J. F. Dölger (ed.), *Konstantin der Grosse und seine Zeit*, Freiburg: 1913, 143–154

Levi, M. A., 'La campagna da Costantino nell'Italia settentrionale' in *Bolletino storico-bibliografico subalpino* 36 (1934), 1–10

Messineo, G., 'La Via Flaminia tra V e VI Miglio' in R. Pergola (ed.), *Suburbium. Il suburbia di Roma dalla crisi del sisterna delle ville a Gregorio Magno*, Rome: 2003, 25–46

Moltke, H. von, *Wanderbuch: Handschriftliche Aufzeichnungen aus dem Reisetagebuch*, 4th ed. Berlin: 1879

Moreau, J., 'Pont Milvius ou Saxa Rubra?' in *Nouvelle Clio* 4 (1952), 369–373 = J. Moreau, *Sripta Minora*, Heidelberg: 1964, 72–75

Nibby, A., *Analisi storico-topografico-antiquaria della carta de' Dintorni di Roma*, vol. III. Rome: 1837

Odahl, C., 'An Eschatological Interpretation of Constantine's Labarum Coin' in *Society for Ancient Numismatics* 6.3 (1975), 47–51

Panella, C. (ed.), *I Segni del Potere. Realtà e Immaginario della Sovranità nella Roma Imperiale*, Rome: 2011

Paschoud, F. (ed.), Zosime, *Histoire Nouvelle*, Livres I–II. Paris: 1971

Ritterling, E. 'Legio' in *Realencyclopädie der klassischen Altertumswissenschaft* 12 (1924–25), 1211–1829

Rossi, D. (ed.), *Sulla via Flaminia: Il mausoleo di Marco Nonio Macrino*, Rome: 2012

Seeck, O., *Geschichte des Untergangs der Antiken Welt*, vol. I, 4th ed. Stuttgart: 1921

Seston, W., *Scripta Varia*, Rome: 1980

Smith, A. S., *The Tiber and Its Tributaries: Their Natural History and Classical Associations*, London: 1877
Speidel, M. P., '*Catafractarii Clibanarii* and the Rise of Later Roman Mailed Cavalry' in *Epigraphica Anatolica* 4 (1984), 151–156 = Speidel 1992a, 406–413
Speidel, M. P., 'Maxentius and his *Equites Singulares* at the Battle of the Milvian Bridge' in *Classical Antiquity* 5 (1986), 253–262 = Speidel 1992a, 272–289
Speidel, M. P., 'The Later Roman Field Army and the Guard of the High Empire' in *Latomus* 46 (1987), 375–379 = Speidel 1992a, 379–384
Speidel, M. P., 'Maxentius' Praetorians' in Speidel 1992a, 385–389
Speidel, M. P., *Roman Army Studies, vol. II* (Mavors 8), Stuttgart: 1992a
Speidel, M. P., *The Framework of an Imperial Legion*, Caerleon: 1992b. A revised version appears in R. J. Brewer (ed.), *The Second Augustan Legion and the Roman Military Machine*, Cardiff: 2002, 125–43
Speidel, M. P., *Riding for Caesar*, Cambridge, Mass.: 1994a
Speidel, M. P., *Die Denkmäler der Kaiserreiter. Equites Singulares Augusti*, Cologne: 1994b
Speidel, M. P., 'Raising New Units for the Late Roman Army: *Auxilia* Palatina' in *Dumbarton Oaks Papers* 50 (1996), 163–170
Speidel, M. P., 'Who Fought in the Front?' in G. Alföldy et al. (eds), *Kaiser, Heer und Gesellschaft in der Römischen Kaiserzeit*, Stuttgart: 2000, 473–482
Speidel, M. P., *Emperor Hadrian's Speeches to the African Armies – A New Text*, Mainz: 2006
Starr, C. G., *The Roman Imperial Navy, 31 BC – AD 324*, 2nd ed. Cambridge: 1960
Toebelmann, F., *Der Bogen von Malborghetto*, Heidelberg: 1915
Trombley, F., 'Ammianus Marcellinus and Fourth-Century Warfare: A Protector's Approach to Historical Narrative' in J. W. Drijvers & D. Hunt (eds), *The Late Roman World and Its Historian: Interpreting Ammianus Marcellinus*, London: 1999
Vistoli, F. (ed.), *La riscoperta della via Flaminia più vicina a Roma: storia, luoghi, personaggi*, Rome: 2010
Wellesley, K., *The Year of the Four Emperors*, 3rd ed. London: 2000

ABBREVIATIONS

AE	L'Année Épigraphique
Chrest. Mitt.	Grundzüge und Chrestomathie der Papyruskunde
CIL	Corpus Inscriptionum Latinarum
IK	Inschriften Griechischer Städte aus Kleinasien
ILS	Inscriptiones Latinae Selectae
Pais	E. Pais (ed.), Corporis Inscriptionum Latinarum Supplementa Italica. Rome: 1884
P.Col.	Columbia Papyri
P.Beatty.	Panop. T. C. Skeat (ed.), Papyri from Panopolis in the Chester Beatty Library, Dublin. Dublin: 1964
P.Lond.	Greek Papyri in the British Museum
P.Oxy.	Oxyrhynchus Papyri
RIC	Roman Imperial Coinage
Amm. Marc.	Ammianus Marcellinus
Arr. Ect.	Arrian, Expedition against the Alans
Aur. Vict.	Aurelius Victor
Caes. BG; BC	Caesar, Gallic War; Civil War
Chr. Min. I T.	Mommsen (ed.), Chronica Minora saec. IV. V. VI. VII., vol. I. Berlin: 1892
Cic. Cat.	Cicero, Catiline
Cod. Just.	Justinianic Code
Cod. Theod.	Theodosian Code
Dio	Cassius Dio
Epit.	Epitome of the Caesars
Euseb.	HE; VCEusebius, Ecclesiastical History; Life of Constantine
Eutrop.	Eutropius
Fest. Brev.	Festus, Breviarium
FGrHDie	Fragmente der Griechischen Historiker
HA Sev.	Historia Augusta, Severus
Hdn	Herodian
Jul. Or.	Julian, Orations
Lact. DMP	Lactantius, On the Deaths of the Persecutors
Lib. Or.	Libanius, Orations
Lib. Pont.	Book of the Pontiffs
Liv.	Livy
Mart. Epigr.	Martial, Epigrams
Maur. Strat.	Maurice, Strategicon
Not. Dig.	Notitia Dignitatum
Oratio	Constantine, Oration to the Saints
Origo	The Origin of Constantine
Ov. Pont.	Ovid, Black Sea Letters
Pan. Lat.	Latin Panegyrics
Pl. NH	Pliny, Natural History
Polyb.	Polybius
Strab. Geog.	Strabo, Geography
Suet. Ner.	Suetonius, Nero
Tac. Ann.; Hist.	Tacitus, Annals; Histories
Veg.	Vegetius
Zon.	Zonaras
Zos.	Zosimus

INDEX

Africa 6, 11, 13, 24
agmen quadratum formation 58, 80, 81, 85
Alexander, Domitius 11, 12–13, 24
Allia, Battle of the (390 BC) **62**
Apollo Grannus (Grand) sanctuary 13, 15
Aquileia 39, 40, **77**
Arch of Constantine, the 49–56, **85, 87, 88**
Arch of Malborghetto, the **61,** 62
archaeology of the Milvian Bridge region 66–72
Ariminum (Rimini) 41
armatura 20
armour 31, **31, 52,** 56, **72**
army strength
    Constantine's army 17–18, 20, 21, 65, 77
    Maxentius' army 23–24, 47, 65, 77
Asclepiodotus 18
Asiana 6, 15
Augusta Taurinorum 35, 36, **36,** 37, **37,** 77
Augustus 6–7
Aulucentius, Valerius **28**
auxilia 22–23
axes 31, **31**

Bagaudae campaign (AD 285) 18
Baudio, Florius 41–43, **43**
Bitus, Aurelius 24
bows 31
Britannia 6, 19
Brixia (Brescia) 38, 77

Caesar, Julius 29
Caesars, The (Victor) 61–64
Carausius 18
Carnuntum (Petronell) 12
Carpi, the 13
Castra Praetoria, the 19, 87
centuriae (centuries) 28
Christogram, the 48, 49, **52,** 57, **58, 59, 72,** 77
chronology 16
clubs 36
comites Augustorum nostrorum 19
Constantine **13, 32** *see also*
    Constantine's army
    aftermath 86–89
    becomes Augustus 12, 15
    becomes Caesar 7, **7**
    campaign against the Picts 6–7
    chronology 16
    commemorative medallion **58, 59,** 59–60
    dreams and visions 13–14, 15, 48, 57, 77
    early career 5–6
    enters Rome 88–89
    his role as commander 32–33
    marries the daughter of Maximian 11
    religion 14, 48, 57, **58,** 59–60, 77
Constantine's army 44–66
    the advance on Rome 41–43
    armour 31, **31**
    auxilia and *vexillationes* 22–23
    Battle of the Milvian Bridge (AD 312) **54–55, 72,** 73–85
    Brixia and Verona 38–40
    commanders 23
    construction projects 22
    formations 36, 40, 81
    guardsmen 17–20
    helmets 22, **73**
    legions 21–22
    morale 36
    musicians 56
    primary sources on the battle 44–66
    Segusio to Augusta Taurinorum 34–38
    shields **52, 72**
    siege of Verona 20, 38–40
    standards **35, 52,** 57
    strength 17–18, 20, 21, 65, 77
    tactical organization 28–31
    weapons 20, 28, 30, 31, **31,** 36, **72**
Constantius 5, **5,** 6, **6,** 7
Corsica 11
Crescentianus, Aurelius 37, **37,** 43
cuneus (wedge) formation 35–36

Daia, Maximinus 20
darts 28
deserters 24–25
Diocletian 5, **5,** 6, 7, 12, 19, 20, 22, **22**
Dizon, Valerius 26
double battle line formation 40, 81
dreams and visions 13–14, 15, 48, 57, 77

duplex acies (double battle line) formation 40, 81

Ecclesiastical History (Eusebius) 56–57
Edict of Milan 89
Epitome de Caesaribus 64–65
Eporedia (Ivrea) 35, 36, 37
equites promoti dominici 25
equites singulares Augusti (Imperial Horse Guards) 8, 18, **18,** 19, 23, 26, 31, **84,** 87
Eunapius 65
Eusebius 56–57

Fausta 11
Faustus, Aurelius 48
Florentius, Valerius 40
forfex (forceps) formation 36
formations 29, 30
    Constantine's army 36, 40, 81
    Maxentius' army 35–36, 58, 80, 81, 85
four-sided column formation 58, 80, 81, 85

Galeria Maximilla 7
Galerius **5,** 5–6, 7, 9–11, **10,** 12, 13, 14–15, **15,** 19, **19**
Gaul 6
Genialis, Valerius 43
Gentiles, the 20
German legions 21
Great Persecution of the Christians, the 48–49
Great Trajanic Frieze, the 60
guardsmen 17–20, **18, 19,** 86–88

Hadrian, Emperor 29
Hannibal 81
helmets 22, **52, 58, 73**
Herodius, Valerius 40
Hispania 6
Histria (Istira) 12
horse guardsmen, the 7, 8, 86–88

Ienuarius, Valerius 36–37, **37**
Ingenuus, Klaudius 23
Issus, Battle of (AD 194) 63
Iulianus, Aurelius 26
Iustinus, Aurelius 29, **30**
Iustinus, Valerius 43

javelins 20, 25, **27**, 28, 30, **72**

Lactantius 47–49
lances 31
Latin Panegyric, the 44–47, 58–60, 61–62
legio II Parthica 26
Libanius 61
Licinius 12, **12**, 13, 14–15, 44, 89
Life of Constantine (Eusebius) 57
Lingonica (Langres) 6
Lucianus 7
Lugunum, Battle of (AD 197) 63

maces 31
Macrinus, Nonius 69
Marcellianus 7
Marcellinus, Ammianus 48
Marcellus 7
Marcianus, Aurelius 37, **37**
Marcus 37
Martinus, Aurelius 18
Mauri, the 20, 24, 26, 31, **39**, 76
Maxentius 33 *see also* Maxentius' army
  chronology 16
  on Constantine becoming Caesar 7
  and Constantine's invasion of Italy 34–38
  death of 47, 49, 59, 60, 65, 66
  and Domitius Alexander 12–13
  early career 6, 9
  his role as commander 33
  massacre in Rome 11
  proclaimed *princeps* 7, 8
  regalia 45
  Rome's defences 45
  and Severus 9
  victory over Galerius 10–11
Maxentius' army
  armour 31, **31**, **52**, 56, **72**
  Battle of the Milvian Bridge (AD 312) 44–66, **54–55**, **72**, 73–85
  Brixia and Verona 38–40, 77
  and Constantine's advance on Rome 41–43
  deserters 24–25
  formations 35–36, 58, 80, 81, 85
  legio II Parthica 26
  naval power 23–24
  praetorians 24–25, 77, 86–88
  primary sources on the battle 44–66
  protectores 25
  remansores 23–24
  shields **72**

standards **52**, **72**
strength 23–24, 47, 65, 77
tactical organization 28–31
urban cohorts 23, 24
weapons 25, 28, 30, 31, **31**
Maximian **5**, 5–6, 8, **8**, 9, 11, 12, 13, 14, 18
Maximinus 6, **6**, 15, 19, 89
Maximus, Aurelius 37, **37**
Mediolanum (Milan) 6, 38
Mesopotamia 26
Modestus, Ladinus 68
Moesia 6
Mucianus, Aurelius **26**
musicians 28, **52**, 56
Mutina (Modena) 40, 77

naval power, Maxentius' army 23–24
Nazarius 58–60
New History (Zosimus) 65–66
Nicomedia (Izmet) 5, 19
Numidians, the 81

On the Deaths of the Persecutors (Lactantius) 47–49
Oriens 6
Origin of Constantine, The 60
Ovid 66, 68

Pannonia 6, 12
Persia, defeat of (AD 298) 32
Persian Empire, the 6
Persian War (AD 298) 26
Picts, the 6–7
plumbatae **81**
Pompeianus, Ruricius 38–39, 40
Pontica 6
praefectus (prefect) 23
praepositi 23
praetorians, the 7, 8, 9, **17**, 17–20, **18**, **19**, 23, 24–25, 26, 47, **72**, 77, 86–88
primary sources 44–66
Primus, Antonius 66
protectores 20, 25

Ravenna 5
Redemtus, Caristicus 68
remansores 23–24
Rivoli 35
Romana Palatina 25, **25**
Romulus 7

Sardinia 11, **12**, 13, 24
Sarmatians, the 13
Saturnanus, Valerius 43

Saturninus 18
Saxa Rubra 48, **60**, 61–64, 73
scholae 20
scutarii 20
Segusio (Susa) 34–35, 77
Severus 6, 7, 9, 11, 86
shields **27**, **52**, **72**
Sibylline Books, the 73
Sicily 11
signa see standards
simplex acies (single battle line) formations 40
Spain 21
spears 30
Spoletium (Spoleto) 41
standards 17, **17**, **21**, 28, **35**, **52**, 57, **72**
swords **27**, 28, 30, **72**, **76**

tactical organization 28–31
Tertius, Valerius 24
Tetrarchs, the **5**, 9, 12
Thracia 6
Tor di Quinto **63**, 64, **64**, 65, 66–72, **67**, **68**, **69**, **72**, 76–85, 90–91, **91**
tribuni (tribunes) 8, 23
Tripolitana 6

Ursianus, Valerius 24, 25

Verona, siege of 20, 38–40, 44, 77
vexillationes 22–23
Victor, Aurelius 61–64
Victorinus, Aurelius 37
Vindex, Aurelius 37
visions 13–14, 15, 48, 55, 77
Vitalianus 48
Vitalis, Aurelius 37
Vitellius 66
Volusianus, Rufius 12–13

weapons
  axes 31, **31**
  bows 31
  clubs 36
  darts 28
  javelins 20, 25, **27**, 28, 30, **72**
  lances 31
  maces 31
  plumbatae **81**
  spears 30
  swords **27**, 28, 30, **72**, **76**
wedge formation 35–36

Zosimus 65–66